What the critics say about
THE BEST OF ST. THOMAS AND ST. JOHN, U.S. VIRGIN ISLANDS
and Ms. Acheson's and Mr. Myers's writing:

"Visitors seeking advice on warmer climes can find it in *The Best of St. Thomas and St. John, U.S. Virgin Islands.*"
—Publisher's Weekly

"A near-guarantee of a great trip."
—Independent Publisher

The authors share their "intimate knowledge of hotels, inns, bars, restaurants, shops and attractions."
—Virgin Islands Weekly Journal

"Essential to getting the most out of any trip."
—Midwest Book Review

"A lighthearted guidebook...full of insider tips and recommendations."
—Essentially America

"The absolute best guidebook on St. Thomas and St. John."
—Peter Island Morning Sun

"A valid and nifty guide to wonderful places."
—The Naples Daily News

"Travelers to St. Thomas want to invest in *The Best of St. Thomas and St. John, U.S. Virgin Islands.*"
—Orlando Sentinel

Acheson and Myers are two "of our extraordinary writers."
—Fodor's Caribbean

"I want to be there, wanna go back down
and lie beside the sea there
with a tin cup for a chalice
fill it up with red wine
and I'm chewin' on a honeysuckle vine."
—*Jimmy Buffett*

THE BEST OF ST. THOMAS AND ST. JOHN, U.S. VIRGIN ISLANDS

Third Edition

PAMELA ACHESON
RICHARD B. MYERS

TWO THOUSAND THREE ASSOCIATES
TTTA

Published by
TWO THOUSAND THREE ASSOCIATES
4180 Saxon Drive, New Smyrna Beach, Florida 32169
Phone: 386.423.7523

Library of Congress Cataloging-in-Publication Data
Acheson, Pamela.
  The best of St. Thomas and St. John, U.S. Virgin Islands / Pamela Acheson,
  Richard B. Myers.
  p.   cm.
  Includes index.
  ISBN 13: 9781892285126
  1. Saint Thomas (V.I.)--Guidebooks. 2. Saint John (V.I.)--Guidebooks
  I. Title
  F2105.A64   1998
  917.297'22--dc21   98-48750
                                                             CIP

Printed in the United States of America

Photo Credits
Front Cover: Pamela Acheson. St. Thomas from Caneel Bay, St. John
Back Cover: Pamela Acheson, St. Thomas from Gallows Point, St. John

1SBN-13: 9781892285126
1SBN-10: 1892285126

10 9 8 7 6 5 4

in memory
of
Joyce Keener

who said
"friends, like food and beauty, are essentials"

*A word from the editor about the authors' research
and the timeliness and accuracy of this book:*

The authors have stayed at every lodging choice in this book at least several times. They have eaten in every restaurant in this book many times. They have been to every shop, attraction, museum, etc. They have done all this anonymously.

They pay their own way.

The authors have also been to many resorts, inns, restaurants, bars, and attractions that they chose not to put in this book.

Believe me, the authors have done their homework. And because they have devoted all their efforts to picking the very best and leaving out the rest, they have done your homework for you.

No establishment mentioned in this book has paid to be mentioned. No establishment has written or approved its own description.

Unlike many travel guides, this book finishes its final fact-checking process only three to four weeks before the book is on the shelves in your local bookstore.

The authors' books are the most current books in the industry when they hit the shelves and they are updated regularly.

—H.H.

ACKNOWLEDGMENTS

Special thanks to Jon Corhern at Imagecraft Design.

DISCLAIMER

The authors have made every effort to ensure accuracy in this book but bear in mind that, despite what you hear about the peaceful pace of "island time," everything to do with vacationing in the Caribbean–schedules, restaurants, hotels, events, modes of transportation, etc., can open, relocate, or close with remarkable speed. Neither the authors nor the publisher are responsible for anyone's traveling or vacation experiences.

INTRODUCTION

Altogether there are about 60 islands, islets, and cays in the U.S. Virgin Islands. Most are uninhabited. The four main U.S. Virgin Islands are St. Thomas, little Water Island (just off the south shore of St. Thomas), St. John (two miles east of St. Thomas), and St. Croix, 40 miles to the south.

We love St. Thomas and St. John. Like brothers or sisters, they share similarities and differences. They complement each other, and they stand on their own. Despite their geographical similarities and the fact that they are only two miles apart, in many ways they are two entirely different destinations. Together they offer a mixed U.S. and Caribbean experience.

Although you'll find familiar U.S. staples like traffic jams and Big Macs and large resorts and uniformed park rangers, they're all entwined in an authentic Caribbean setting. You'll also find acres and acres of untouched land, intimate inns, tiny beachfront restaurants, a laid-back style of living, and absolutely spectacular scenery—tropical blue water lapping against classic crescents of white sand, steep green hills, beaches that will steal your heart. It's an "island experience" that is truly unique.

St. John and St. Thomas are U.S. Territories. The language is English (with the delightful island lilt). The currency is U.S. dollars. The flights are frequent. The weather, near perfect.

The two islands are only a 20-minute ferry ride apart and on any day, on either or both of the islands, you can swim or snorkel in the crystal-clear Caribbean, enjoy mountaintop views, some amazing jeep rides or hikes, a world-class dinner, and the glimmering lights on the water, over the water, and even under it.

There is truly something for everyone on these islands and it is our hope that *The Best of St. Thomas and St. John, U.S. Virgin Islands* will help anyone visiting these islands have a more hassle-free, enjoyable, and memorable Virgin Island vacation. So set your mind to island time and enjoy the adventure.

—*P.A. and R.B.M.*

TABLE OF CONTENTS

SPECIAL FEATURES

THE U.S. VIRGIN ISLANDS
IN RELATION TO THE
REST OF THE WORLD

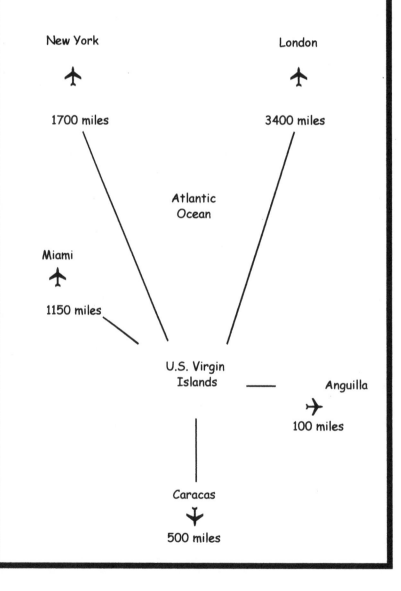

New York

1700 miles

London

3400 miles

Atlantic Ocean

Miami

1150 miles

U.S. Virgin Islands —— Anguilla

100 miles

Caracas

500 miles

SECTION I

ST. THOMAS

PLACES TO STAY
RESTAURANTS
BARS
SHOPPING
LUNCH BREAKS
BEACHES
WATERSPORTS
LANDSPORTS
ISLAND ATTRACTIONS

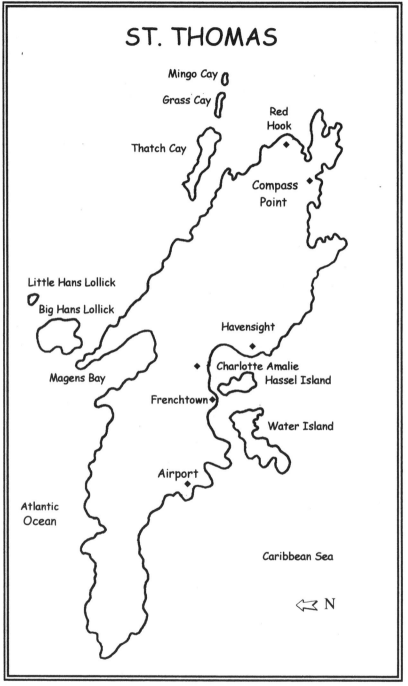

ST. THOMAS

Mingo Cay

Grass Cay

Red Hook

Thatch Cay

Compass Point

Little Hans Lollick

Big Hans Lollick

Havensight

Charlotte Amalie

Hassel Island

Magens Bay

Frenchtown

Water Island

Airport

Atlantic Ocean

Caribbean Sea

N

ABOUT ST. THOMAS

St. Thomas is a hugely popular destination and decidedly cosmopolitan. It's an island of world-class shopping, fine dining, and full-service resorts but it also has its share of traffic jams, honking horns, and cruise ship crowds. The overall atmosphere is lively and active. Restaurants are full and open late, beaches are busy with volleyball games, taxis are packed with people going somewhere, downtown streets are bustling with shoppers, and groups of snorkelers are checking out the underwater sights. On the other hand, you can easily find a quiet bar or an intimate table for two or a peaceful spot at the end of a beach.

St. Thomas is easy to reach (there are nonstop flights from major U.S. cities) and it's an easy place to be. The island offers all the comforts of home, yet it has a true Caribbean soul. It's a great place to go when you want to get away fast to tropical weather, when you want to spend your days at the beach and your nights out and about, when you want to really relax and do nothing, and when you want to be somewhere that is truly Caribbean and somewhat exotic but not totally unfamiliar.

St. Thomas, at 32 square miles, is the largest and most populated U.S. Virgin Island and about 52,000 people live there (whereas only 4,200 people live on the island of St. John, which is two miles to the east). St. Thomas is 13 miles long and its width varies from one to four miles, but this narrowness is deceiving since you almost always have to go up over a steep hill to get to the other side. The island is lushly tropical, rugged, and mountainous and ringed with crescents of white sand. Views from the hills are spectacular.

Most resorts are on the east end of St. Thomas, near Red Hook. Others are near Charlotte Amalie (it's pronounced ah-MAL-yuh). Most restaurants are in Charlotte Amalie, in Frenchtown (which is next to Charlotte Amalie), and out on the east end of the island. Some people think Charlotte Amalie is only for duty-free shoppers, but it also has many one-of-a-kind little shops and even people who hate to shop get smitten. It's also a lovely town. Look for stonework and brick walls, ornate gates and balconies, graceful archways, and colorful doors.

DID YOU KNOW?

❑St. Thomas is on the same geologic shelf as the British Virgin Islands and Puerto Rico. It is thought that several times in the last 60 million years you could probably have walked from one island to another on dry land.

❑St. Thomas is 18 degrees north of the equator.

❑If you headed straight east, you'd cross the British Virgin Islands, the island of Anguilla, and then, about 3,000 miles later, the Cape Verde Islands which are just off the coast of North Africa.

❑If you walked along St. Thomas's curvy coastline until you got back to where you started, you would have walked almost 60 miles.

❑The turpentine tree is quite distinctive looking, with red-orange bark. It's sometimes called the "tourist tree" because its skin is constantly peeling.

❑The machineel tree can be a real pain. It bears small green apples, which are poisonous. Its sap and bark can cause painful blistering that feels just like a bad burn. Don't even stand under the tree in a rain—water dripping from the leaves will burn your skin.

❑The reason there are so many stairs outside in Charlotte Amalie is that the Danes laid out plans for the city back in Denmark and thought the land was flat. When it came time to build, wherever it was just too steep to put a street, they had to build a stairway instead.

CHAPTER 1

GREAT
ST. THOMAS
PLACES
TO STAY

"There is nothing which has yet been
contrived by man by which so much
happiness is produced as by
a good tavern or inn."

—*Samuel Johnson*

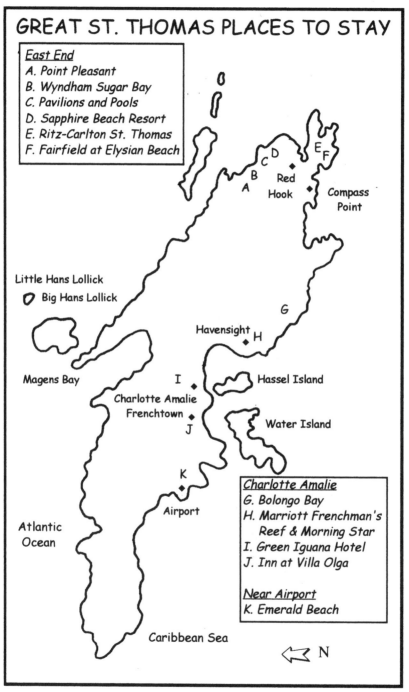

GREAT ST. THOMAS PLACES TO STAY

East End
A. Point Pleasant
B. Wyndham Sugar Bay
C. Pavilions and Pools
D. Sapphire Beach Resort
E. Ritz-Carlton St. Thomas
F. Fairfield at Elysian Beach

Red Hook

Compass Point

Little Hans Lollick

Big Hans Lollick

Havensight

Magens Bay

Hassel Island

Charlotte Amalie
Frenchtown

Water Island

Airport

Atlantic Ocean

Charlotte Amalie
G. Bolongo Bay
H. Marriott Frenchman's
   Reef & Morning Star
I. Green Iguana Hotel
J. Inn at Villa Olga

Near Airport
K. Emerald Beach

Caribbean Sea

N

GREAT ST. THOMAS PLACES TO STAY

There are all kinds of great places to stay on St. Thomas: full-service resorts that you really never ever have to leave, motel-style beachfront hotels, intimate inns, condo-style units with full kitchens, and a wide range of rental villas.

Where you decide to stay on St. Thomas can depend on what you like to do. Do you want to roll out of bed onto the beach, or spend the days visiting different beaches or exploring the island? Do you want to avoid shopping, or shop every day, or maybe just once? Do you want a big, full-service hotel with several restaurants right on the property, or do you want a small inn? Or do you want the privacy of a villa?

Generally speaking, places to stay are either near Charlotte Amalie or about 25 minutes away, along the eastern end of the island. There are advantages to both locations. If you are near Charlotte Amalie, you are close to world-class shopping, many excellent restaurants and tourist attractions, and not that far from famous Magens Bay Beach.

If you choose to stay on the east end of St. Thomas, you are more "out in the country." You are not far from a different set of restaurants and close to the little town of Red Hook, which has limited but interesting shopping. Red Hook is where ferries leave frequently for St. John and the British Virgin Islands (less frequent service is also available from downtown Charlotte Amalie). You are also close to the departure point for many charter boat day trips and you are near a number of very good beaches. At most east end resorts, you will also have stunning views of St. John and the British Virgin Islands in the distance.

Rental villas are scattered all over the island and can be found on the beach and high in the hills. Many overlook beautiful Magens Bay.

This chapter first describes places to stay along the east end of St. Thomas, followed by places near or in Charlotte Amalie. Rates are per night without meals for two people on–season (off-season rates in parentheses) and do not include 8% room tax or hotel service charges.

17

FAIRFIELD AT ELYSIAN BEACH RESORT

What makes this spot special is the combination of excellent service, spacious and contemporary units (many with full kitchens), appealing private grounds, and being perhaps the most central location on the east end of St. Thomas. It's just a mile to the little town of Red Hook and numerous restaurants are within a five- to ten-minute drive.

Four- and five-story buildings, painted bright white, are clustered tightly together on a steep hillside that sweeps down to a long crescent of beach. The 67 deluxe rooms and suites in this time-share property look out past beautifully manicured grounds to a picturesque harbor and St. James Island in the distance. Units are bright and spacious with comfortable whitewashed rattan furnishings, white tile floors, and pastel print fabrics. The suites have full kitchens and terraces, and some are duplexes with spiral staircases leading to a second-floor bedroom loft and a private balcony. All rooms have air-conditioning, TVs, VCRs, safes, and irons.

The free-form swimming pool has a waterfall (check out the secret underwater bench behind it) and the beach is a half-moon of glistening white sand. The use of sailboats, kayaks, pedal boats, beach floats, and snorkel gear are complimentary. Scuba lessons, parasailing, dive and snorkel trips, sailing excursions, boat rentals, and sport fishing trips can be arranged. A tennis court, a health and fitness center, and a large boutique round out the plentiful facilities.

The open-air Robert's American Grill is a pleasant stop for dinner. Guests gather around the piano bar Tuesday through Sunday evenings to listen to piano music from 7 p.m. to 10 p.m., and the thatched-roof beach bar turns out frozen specialty drinks all day long. Bonnie's by the Sea is a very casual restaurant down on the beach that serves breakfast, lunch, and dinner. Friday evenings, there is often a steel drum band.

You never have to leave the property, but if you feel like venturing outside the Elysian, you'll find that you are in one of the best east end locations. Good restaurants are close by in virtually every direction and the town of Red Hook is practically around the corner.

2 restaurants, 2 bars, pool, tennis court, health club and fitness center, watersports center, gift shop. 67 units. $190-$259 all year. Cowpet Bay, 6800 Estate Nazareth, 00802. Res: 800.438.6493. Tel: 340.775.1000. Fax: 340.776.0910. www.elysianbeachresort.net

PAVILIONS AND POOLS

You'll love this place if you have ever dreamed about being able to fall out of bed into your own very private pool—one that you can swim in by the light of the sun or even the moon. It's not a full-service resort and it doesn't have a beach (although one is a short walk away), but it does have complete indoor and outdoor privacy.

Pavilions and Pools is nestled on the east end of St. Thomas on a hill just above Sapphire Beach. Two long, rather ordinary-looking buildings house rows of basically comfortable and very private apartments, each with its own personal swimming pool.

A fenced-in terrace around the pool affords true privacy. All you can see are trees and sky and you are visible to no one, except perhaps a passing bird. You are free to swim or float as naked as you wish, under the noonday sun or gazing up at the midnight stars. These pools are literally right next to both the living room and bedroom area and you can actually step right into the pool from either room, or sit at the edge of the room and dangle your legs in the water.

The units (which are far from plush) and pools come in two sizes. The International features a 20' x 14' pool and 1400 square feet of living space. The Caribbean has a 16' x 18' pool and 1200 square feet of living space. All units have an air-conditioned bedroom, living room, and full kitchen, plus a shower nestled against a sunken garden. The larger units have a dining area and walk-in closets and a bigger shower-garden area. All units have a TV and VCR, safe, and an iron.

This is a fine place to completely relax. An informal little brick and stone honor bar is open from 8 a.m. to 9 p.m. Continental breakfast is served here daily and so is a simple dinner (two entrees nightly) Wednesday through Sunday 6 p.m to 9 p.m. Or you can cook your own meal and have a romantic starlight dinner by your private pool. Many restaurants (and an excellent grocery store) are five minutes away and there's a daily shuttle into Charlotte Amalie. There's a video library and maid service is available every third day.

Continental breakfast included in the rate, dinner restaurant with limited menu, private pools. Excellent special packages. 25 units, all with pools. $250-$275 ($180-$195). 6400 Estate Smith Bay Rd., 00802. Res: 800.524.2001. Tel and fax: 340.775.6110. www.pavilionsandpools.com

POINT PLEASANT RESORT

This waterfront resort is scattered up the side of a steep hill and nestled in dense greenery. Come here if you want a full kitchen, you love great views, and like to walk on winding, woodsy trails. The shore is rocky and the beaches minuscule but the pools here are superb and there's a long beach next door.

You'd never know there are 128 units in this resort. One- to four-story, red-roofed buildings are surrounded by trees and discreetly tucked here and there in the steep hillside. Great care has been taken not to disturb the environment. Narrow paths (some fairly steep) and wooden walkways lead from building to building, pool to pool, to reception and the restaurants, and off into the woods. An occasional bench or hammock along the walks beckons one to rest.

The apartment-like units have wide expanses of glass that show off the view and many have giant terraces. Generally, the higher up you are, the more spectacular the scenery. You can choose a studio, or one bedroom, or two bedrooms. All are air-conditioned and have full kitchens, TVs, safes (for a fee), and irons. Decor varies, as these are individually owned units, but rooms are generally simply furnished. Those who want the convenience (or pleasure) of a full kitchen, a wide terrace for sunning and stargazing, woodsy paths to hike, and stunning views will find this a very pleasant choice.

The Agave Terrace, one of the east end's most popular seafood restaurants *(see page 38)*, sits on the hillside near reception. Fungi's on the Beach is an ultracasual waterside stop for lunch, snacks, and dinner. Three spectacular pools are at different levels with different views. Amazingly, you can almost always find an empty one—people who stay here seem to be off doing things—and don't be surprised if an iguana wanders by to take a look at you while you are sunning. The watersports center offers complimentary windsurfers, snorkel equipment, kayaks, and little sailboats. There's a small exercise room and an Activities Desk.

The resort is a five-minute ride from Red Hook and a number of popular restaurants, and it's a short walk to a good swimming beach.

2 restaurants, 2 bars, 3 pools, shop. Packages. 128 units (80 available for rent). $255-$275 ($180-$195). 6600 Smith Bay Rd., 00802. Res: 800.524.2300 or 800.777.1700. Tel: 340.775.7200. Fax: 340.776.5694. www.pointpleasantresort.com

RITZ-CARLTON, ST. THOMAS

There is no question that this is the most luxurious resort in the U.S. Virgin Islands and one of the best in the Caribbean. A $40 million renovation makes it sparkle. When you want exceptional comfort and service, superb meals in elegant settings, and stunning views, this is the place to come.

A gracious brick driveway lined with a profusion of brilliantly colored tropical flowers leads to the formal entrance of this replica of a Venetian palace. It's not until you reach the registration desk, though, that your gaze is drawn to a window and you get your first real look at this magnificent resort—Italian villa-style buildings facing the sea and, sweeping down to an exquisite pool, is what can only be called "perfect planting." Walkways meander through beautifully manicured lawns and blossoming trees.

The rooms are classic Ritz-Carlton, plush and very civilized. Upholstered sofas provide a comfortable seating area. Wide French or sliding doors open onto a private balcony when you want sunlight and views. Heavy draperies shut out light for sleep. In some rooms the comfortable king-size bed is perfectly positioned so you can lie and look straight out at the sea. (Some rooms have two queens.) There are TVs with in-room movies, a safe, iron, coffee maker, and robes. The spacious marble bathrooms are luxurious for the Caribbean. A separate building houses four floors of Club Floor Suites, plus the Club Lounge and five daily food presentations.

The air-conditioned and elegant Great Bay Grill (*see page 40*) (collared shirt required for men) serves dinner Tuesday through Saturday plus Sunday brunch. The Palm Garden Cafe offers a more casual atmosphere for breakfast, lunch, and dinner. For barefoot dining, try poolside Iguana's for lunch or Coconut Cove, the poolside restaurant at the adjacent Ritz-Carlton fractional ownership club, for lunch and dinner. Both restaurants have a bar. Guests also gather in the Living Room for cigars and brandy.

The pool is stunning, with a view that looks out over its "disappearing edge" to distant islands. There is a half-mile of beach, three tennis courts, a health club and spa, and shopping shuttles to Charlotte Amalie. Several upscale boutiques sell sportswear and a 53' catamaran goes on daily sails.

4 restaurants, 5 bars, 24-hour room service, 2 pools, 2 beaches, 3 tennis courts, health club, spa, shops. Special packages. 200 units. $369-$499, suites more ($319-$389). 6900 Great Bay, 00802. Res: 800.241.3333. Tel: 340.775.3333. Fax: 340.775.4444. www.ritzcarlton.com

SAPPHIRE BEACH RESORT AND MARINA

A half-mile crescent of white sand, turquoise waters, and a view of St. John and the British Virgin Islands in the distance provide an exquisite setting for this casual, full-service resort that is popular with families.

Don't worry that the entrance is less than grand. A driveway swings down through somewhat unkempt foliage to an unassuming yellow building and other than the distant view of islands, there isn't much to see. But walk through and you're bound to like the superb beach and stunning view.

The beach is exceptionally wide and accommodations are in a number of tin-roofed, four-story buildings at the far edge of the sand. Units are casually and simply decorated but quite comfortable. The entrance leads past a bathroom through the bedroom to a living room with a sleeper sofa and seating arrangement, a dining table, and a full kitchen along one wall. A wide balcony that is perfect for lounging day and night looks across the beach to distant islands. All units have TVs, safes, and are air-conditioned.

Tables at the Windies, the main restaurant, sit under umbrellas on a terrace overlooking the beach and open to the breezes. Nearby is a circular beach bar, open all day and at night the site for weekend entertainment. The Steakhouse at the Point is open for dinner on-season.

The half-mile-long beach curves around the bay in a sweeping arc and is good for walking as well as sunning. Hammocks are strung here and there. While the two ends of the beach are less crowded and it can be possible to find a spot by yourself under a sea grape tree, the center of the beach tends to be busy, particularly at the volleyball court and around the watersports center, which offers complimentary snorkeling, sunfish sailing, and windsurfing. There is a charge for parasailing and renting waverunners. The watersports center can also arrange sport fishing and sailing trips. An on-site full-service PADI dive center offers certification programs and diving trips. Handcrafted stone walls and a glassy waterfall separate the two tiers of the gorgeous pool which is out on a point at the end of the beach. Guest services offer a huge array of activities at the resort—crab races, sand castle contests, tennis clinics—and also around the island, from sunset sails to tours of St. Thomas.

3 restaurants, 2 bars, pool, beach, 4 tennis courts. Special packages. 171 units. $335-$495 ($225-325). P.O. Box 8088, 00801. Res: 800.524.2090. Tel: 340.775.6100. Fax: 340.775.2403. www.usvi.net/hotel/sapphire

WYNDHAM SUGAR BAY RESORT & SPA

This is an absolutely all-inclusive, full-service resort and just about everything really is included. Eat, drink, play tennis, go windsurfing, bring your children in the summer—all at no additional charge.

Staying here is almost like going on a cruise but knowing you don't have to worry about getting seasick. Virtually everything is included in the room price: all meals and snacks (you can eat here all day long), all drinks including wine, champagne, and premium brand liquors during bar hours (which are extensive); use of all nonmotorized boats; daily activities; classes; and evening entertainment.

Rooms are in two tiers of rather imposing three-story buildings that crown a small hill. They are large and comfortably furnished, and have private balconies. Some have stunning views of nearby islands, others catch the bay, and others look out to the pool and up into hills. Rooms have coffee maker, fridge, safe, a TV with in-room movies, and air-conditioning.

From 7 a.m until 11 p.m. there's always food available. Tuscany's, open nightly, offers Italian specialties in a romantic atmosphere. The Manor House serves a buffet breakfast, for dinner switches from a la carte to themed buffets, and also has a late-night menu. The casual, poolside Mangrove restaurant offers a lunch buffet daily and themed dinner buffets. Hot dogs, hamburgers, grilled fish, and other goodies are available at a poolside grill from noon to 5 p.m. You can always find a bar open from 11 a.m. to 1 a.m. Nightly entertainment features live bands, karaoke, and DJs.

It's a steep drop (via stairs or elevator) down to the pool and beach area. A swinging bridge crosses over free-form pools with great waterfalls you can swim under and hide behind. There's a small beach where you can snorkel, sunfish, windsurf, take out a Hobie Cat or a catamaran, or just lie back and relax. (You can also walk around the rocks, when the water is calm, to the trail to Water Bay Beach.) Scheduled activities run day and night (power walks, bingo, movies). Castaways is a superb shop in the lobby. If you find time to leave, Red Hook is minutes away. The two-story luxury Journeys Spa features just about every treatment imaginable.

2 restaurants, 3 bars, 3 pools with waterfalls, beach, 5 tennis courts, basketball, beach volleyball, fitness center, shop. 300 units. $575-$660 ($485-$545) all-inclusive. 6500 Estate Smith Bay, 00802. Res: 800.WYNDHAM (800.996.3426). Tel: 340.777.7100. Fax: 340.777.7200. www.wyndham.com

MARRIOTT FRENCHMAN'S REEF & MORNING STAR

These two sister resorts, Frenchman's Reef and Morning Star, are at the opposite ends of the same property and share the same facilities. Together they form a sparkling gem of a complete, full-service resort that you just never, ever have to leave.

Frenchman's Reef and Morning Star are two completely different places to stay. Frenchman's Reef is a huge, eight-story hotel, along with several multistory wings, perched dramatically on a cliff. Several duty-free shops, a fitness center, a deli, two swimming pools, and bars and restaurants are also located here. Rooms are spacious and stateside-like. Most have excellent ocean views, some look out over the harbor (which is also pretty), and a few get only sky and parking lot. Garden View rooms are larger than Ocean View rooms, but have no balcony. The top level consists of 22 two-story suites. The pool, complete with cascading waterfalls, fountains, Jacuzzis, and a swim-up bar, overlooks the harbor. You'll want to choose Frenchman's Reef if you want to be close to everything and don't mind not being right on the beach.

Morning Star Resort is the place to stay if you want to fall out of your bed right onto the sand. The 96 rooms here are in a series of small three-story buildings that line the beach and are either oceanfront, ocean view, or garden view. Units are decorated in tropical decor and have large terraces or balconies. There are two restaurants and bars close by and a large pool right at the end of the beach. Each resort has its own check-in desk (be sure to tell the taxi driver which resort you are going to), and all rooms have a safe, TV with movies, and coffee maker.

Choose from two lunch restaurants, four dinner restaurants (*including the immensely popular Havana Blue, see page 48*), and five bars. There are tennis courts, a health spa with state-of-the-art exercise equipment and numerous therapeutic massage and skin care treatments, and a watersports center; snorkeling, sailing, parasailing, and scuba diving trips can all be arranged. Shoppers can spend time in one of the on-site shops, or catch the ferry that makes daily trips to Charlotte Amalie (*see page 141*).

6 restaurants, 5 bars, 24-hour room service (7 a.m.-11 p.m.), 3 pools, beach, 2 tennis courts, watersports center, health club/spa, 24-hour deli/market. 481 units. $350-$620, suites more ($159-$211). P.O. Box 7100, Charlotte Amalie, 00801. Res: 800.223.6388. Tel: 340.776.8500. Fax: 340.715.6193. www.marriott.vi

BOLONGO BAY BEACH RESORT

This friendly, family owned and run all-inclusive resort has everything you could want in a Caribbean vacation. Once you get there, you'll find no reason to leave.

This casual, mid-sized beach resort is one of St. Thomas's perennial favorites. And although the resort offers an optional European plan, the all-inclusive option can't be beat. All imaginable water sports, plus tennis, volleyball, basketball, and a la carte meals at your choice of the fine dining Beach House restaurant or the more casual Iggie's are included. So are cocktails, beer, and soft drinks. If you stay for a week, they'll even throw in a day sail and a cocktail cruise. Tough to beat.

The 65 rooms are tucked in the palm trees along a beautiful, 1,000-yard beach. All rooms have a terrace or balcony facing the Caribbean and are simply decorated with wicker, rattan, and colorful Caribbean prints. All rooms have air-conditioning, TV, refrigerators, and a safe.

There is a beautiful freshwater pool which is actually wifi if you are crazy enough to bring your laptop. And if you are without your computer but need to check e-mail or log on for any reason there is an Internet kiosk at your disposal.

2 restaurants, 2 bars, pool, beach, tennis courts, fitness center, St. Thomas Dive Club (a 5-star PADI facility). 65 units. $514-$544 ($445-$475) all-inclusive; $270-$300 ($414-$444) EP. Res: 800.766.2840. Tel: 340.775.1800. Fax: 340.775.3208. www.bolongobay.com

EMERALD BEACH RESORT

This casual, convenient Best Western is very close to the airport. It's sort of like a stateside Best Western but with a beautiful pool and beach.

All the rooms at this three-story hotel are beachfront and comfortable, and all have safes, small refrigerators, coffee makers, irons, and data ports. A watersports center offers windsurfers, sailfish, ocean kayaks, and snorkel gear. There is a beach bar and an open-air restaurant for breakfast, lunch, and dinner. This is also a good one-night stop for very late or early flights.

Restaurant, bar, pool, watersports. 90 units. $209-$299 ($149-$189). 8070 Lindbergh Bay, 00802. Res: 800.233.4936. Tel: 340.777.8800. Fax: 340.776.3426. www.emeraldbeach.com

THE GREEN IGUANA HOTEL

This tiny island hotel perched above Charlotte Amalie on Blackbeard's Hill offers comfortable rooms in a relaxed setting and with pretty views at a very comfortable rate.

The Green Iguana hotel has no pool, no beach you can walk to, and no restaurant. What this niche hotel does have are clean, comfortable rooms with TV, air conditioning, refrigerator, microwave, toaster oven, coffee maker, dishes and utensils, and a very central location. You can walk to downtown or drive or taxi to all St. Thomas beaches and attractions.

9 units. $129-$159 ($89-$129). 37B Blackbeard's Hill, 00802. Res: 800.484.8634 (plus pin 9795). Tel: 340.776.7654. Fax: 340.777.4312. www.thegreeniguana.com

INN AT VILLA OLGA

This affordable and very peaceful "in town" inn is within walking distance of Charlotte Amalie and all of Frenchtown's great restaurants.

The twelve guest rooms here are simply furnished, neat, and clean. The four ocean view rooms have private balconies and look out to Water Island and the Caribbean Sea while the eight harbor view rooms look across the St. Thomas harbor to Charlotte Amalie, and showcase distant cruise ships by day and sparkling nighttime scenes.

All rooms have air-conditioning, cable TV, coffee makers, refrigerators and microwaves. The caring managment and quiet, pretty pool make this a fine "home base" from which to explore the island. A small secluded beach is just a short hike away, and as an added bonus Villa Olga guests are welcomed at Bolongo Bay Beach Resort *(see page 25).*

Be warned that this inn is built against a hill. Although this makes for great views, the guest rooms and even the pool are up a flight or two of stairs. However, you'll be packing your walking shoes anyway because everything from world-class shopping, to great restaurants, to the BVI ferry docks are within walking distance of this simple Caribbean inn.

Pool. 12 Units. $125-$150 ($100-$125). 3700 Villa Olga, 00802. Res: 800.524.4746. Tel: 340.715.0900. Fax: 340.715.0843. www.bolongobay.com/villaolga.htm

RENTING A VILLA OR CONDO

Some people think renting a villa is incredibly expensive, that villas are truly luxurious and only for the "rich and famous." Actually they are available in a wide range of sizes and prices, and many are competitive with resort rates.

Villas are wonderful if you would like the convenience of a house—privacy, space, a full kitchen. Some families love them because everyone can "hang out" together around their own private pool (or in the kitchen, just the way they do at home).

Off-season, special lower rates and packages make even big fancy villas affordable, especially if several couples share in the cost or you have a large family. Smaller villas can be a romantic way to celebrate an anniversary. One of the advantages to renting a villa on St. Thomas is location. While most resorts are located on the east and south sides of the island, villas are scattered all over: near beautiful Magens Bay or up in the hills, with unbeatable, airplane-like views of neighboring islands.

Southwind *is a true luxury villa overlooking St. Thomas Harbor with everything from its own private pool to room for 10 to 12. Tel: 215.242.8042, 267.760.4800. www.southwind.vi*

*One of the best sources for villas is **McLaughlin Anderson Luxury Villas**. 1000 Blackbeard's Hill, 00802. Res: 800.537.6246. Tel: 340.776.0635. Fax: 340.777.4737. www.mclaughlinanderson.com. Another choice is **Blue Escapes**, 101 West 6th, Suite 503, Austin, TX 78701. Tel: 800.556.4801, 512.472.8832. Fax: 512.233.5821. www.BlueEscapes.com*

Also check the Island Marketplace and Vacation Rental Guide in the back of each issue of **Caribbean Travel & Life**. *Buy an issue or call 800.588.1689 for a subscription.*

STUFF PEOPLE USUALLY WISH THEY HAD KNOWN SOONER

CHARLOTTE AMALIE AND A BEACH

If you are staying near downtown Charlotte Amalie or shopping there and also want to spend some time at a beach, an easy and enjoyable way to reach a beach is to catch "The Reefer," the little ferry that runs between the waterfront and Marriott Frenchman's Reef Hotel (which is on Morningstar Beach). The ferry leaves from the downtown waterfront. You can usually find it across from Bumpa's and Down Island Trader. The trip takes about 15 minutes and costs $5. Beware that, once you reach the Marriott, a long and steep set of stairs leads up to the hotel and a more gentle path down to the beach. *See page 141 for ferry schedule.*

CHARLOTTE AMALIE HOSPITALITY LOUNGE

When you want an indoor pay phone, a rest room, information about hotels or restaurants or attractions or boat trips, head to the Visitors' Hospitality Lounge. You can also leave luggage here for a small fee per bag. And they showcase a great selection of local art. It's the blue building on the corner of Waterfront Highway and Tolbad Gade *(see map page 65)*. This place is run entirely by volunteers, so please leave a small donation if you can. *340.777.1153*

ST. JOHN, ST. CROIX, AND THE BRITISH VIRGIN ISLANDS

It is really easy to head over to one of these islands for a day and it can be a great adventure, so build it into your schedule. Each island is different, so choose the one you think you'll like the most or take a boat trip and see several. For more specific information, see pages 52-53 for St. Croix, page 94 for the BVI, and page 77 for an evening on St. John (as well as the entire section on St. John, which begins on page 97).

THINGS TO NOTICE
ON ST. THOMAS

The tourists who didn't pack a carry-on.
They are the ones strolling the beach in their
city clothes, sleeves rolled up.

The green flash
as the sun settles into the Caribbean.

Shooting stars and satellites—if you gaze at the night sky
for 15 minutes, you'll see at least one. Guaranteed.

How close the stars look—as if you could just
reach out and touch them.

Phosphorescence lighting up the night sea.

The delightful donkey at Drake's Seat.

Iguanas—they are a little ugly but they know
how to relax.

Beautiful hummingbirds hanging around
the hibiscus blossoms.

MONEY-SAVING HINTS

❏Traveling to and staying in St. Thomas or St. John in the "off season" can save you up to about 40%.

❏No matter what time of the year you are traveling always inquire about any special packages that might be available.

❏In comparing the cost of lodging choices, be sure you are comparing apples to apples. Some room rates might include a continental breakfast or a full breakfast or no breakfast or free watersports. Know what you are paying for.

❏Ask what meal plans and meal options are available.

❏Also ask what "taxes" and service charges and surcharges will be added to your lodging bill. You don't want a 20% surprise at the end of your stay.

❏Calls home to the States from your hotel room may cost substantially more than a nearby pay phone, a special USA Direct line, or even your own cell phone. Check it out before you dial.

❏To avoid any possible problem always agree on the total cost of a taxi ride before you leave and the total cost of a rental or charter before you sign up.

CHAPTER 2

GREAT ST. THOMAS RESTAURANTS

"Part of the secret of success in life
is to eat what you like and
let the food fight it out inside."
—*Mark Twain*

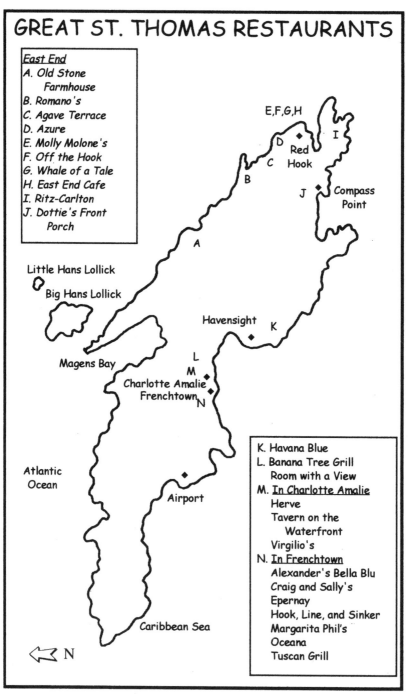

GREAT ST. THOMAS RESTAURANTS

East End
A. Old Stone
    Farmhouse
B. Romano's
C. Agave Terrace
D. Azure
E. Molly Molone's
F. Off the Hook
G. Whale of a Tale
H. East End Cafe
I. Ritz-Carlton
J. Dottie's Front
    Porch

E,F,G,H

I

D

C

Red
Hook

B

J

Compass
Point

A

Little Hans Lollick

Big Hans Lollick

Havensight

K

Magens Bay

L

M

Charlotte Amalie
Frenchtown
N

Atlantic
Ocean

Airport

Caribbean Sea

N

K. Havana Blue
L. Banana Tree Grill
    Room with a View
M. _In Charlotte Amalie_
    Herve
    Tavern on the
        Waterfront
    Virgilio's
N. _In Frenchtown_
    Alexander's Bella Blu
    Craig and Sally's
    Epernay
    Hook, Line, and Sinker
    Margarita Phil's
    Oceana
    Tuscan Grill

GREAT ST. THOMAS RESTAURANTS

St. Thomas is a sophisticated island and has many great restaurants. Some are elegant and some are casual. Some are air-conditioned and indoors and some are open to the Caribbean breezes and look out at great nighttime views. There are many highly skilled chefs on St. Thomas and you can expect to sample some of the best food anywhere. You will find all kinds of cuisine—Italian, German, Continental, Spanish, and West Indian. Local fish to look for on the menu include wahoo, mahi mahi, swordfish, and tuna.

Most restaurants on St. Thomas are either clustered in or near Charlotte Amalie and in Frenchtown (which is just a two-minute cab ride from Charlotte Amalie, on the west side of the St. Thomas Harbor), or they are out on the east end of the island in or near Red Hook. In the evening it's about a 20- to 25-minute ride between the two areas (longer during rush hour). One-way taxi fare is about $10 per person for two or more people. The same taxi that takes you to your restaurant will pick you up also, if you want. Bear in mind that, off-season, hours and days of operation may vary somewhat and it is a good idea to call ahead and check.

DOWNTOWN CHARLOTTE AMALIE RESTAURANTS
HERVE

Dramatic floor-to-ceiling windows capture a stunning view of Charlotte Amalie and the harbor at this delightful hillside restaurant. Relax in delightful air-conditioned comfort and enjoy some of the island's finest cuisine. The menu is not traditionally French, but definitely inspired by the French owners. Tables are very well spaced and elegantly set. Come here for appetizers such as pistachio-crusted brie, warm smoked quail, and classic escargots. Superb dinner choices include lobster, shrimp, and scallop St. Jacques; black-sesame-crusted tuna; grilled lamb chops; and roasted breast of duck. For dessert, try the petite chocolate cups brimming with berries or the rich creme caramel. The wine list is excellent and there are many by the glass. Check out the black and white photographs of St. Thomas back in the gas lamp and horse-and-buggy days. *See page 74 for lunch description. Reservations are a good idea for dinner. No lunch Sun. 340.777.9703. Government Hill. LD $$-$$$*

33

TAVERN ON THE WATERFRONT

This upstairs, air-conditioned restaurant is a welcome retreat from the hustle and bustle below. Windows along the front wall look out across the harbor with cruise ships docked in the distance and sailboats bobbing about. An amusing trompe l'oeil painting looks like a window facing east along Waterfront Highway, but you know it can't be real because there's absolutely no traffic! Romantics may like one of the two private outdoor tables at each end of the dining room. Try the ahi tuna with balsamic onions or almond and hazelnut grouper or spicy baby back pork ribs. *See page 75 for lunch description. Reservations necessary for dinner. Closed Sun. 340.776.4328. Waterfront Hwy. at Royal Dane Mall. LD $$-$$$*

VIRGILIO'S

Exceptional northern Italian cuisine is served indoors in an elegant, intimate atmosphere. Walk into this very dark and cozy air-conditioned restaurant and the rest of the world melts away. Two-story exposed brick walls are hung with a marvelous mix of all sizes of framed paintings and prints. Although tables are quite close together, in most cases, once seated, you forget you have neighbors. The extensive menu offers everything from veal saltimbocca to chicken cacciatore, filet mignon, and capellini with a fresh tomato sauce, plus daily specials. If what you want is not on the menu, do ask. The extensive wine list includes inexpensive wines, but for splurging you can always order the Biondi-Santi Brunello Reserva 1945 for $2,500. End the evening with a tasty Virgilio's cappuccino. *See page 75 for lunch description. Reservations a must. Closed Sun. 340.776.4920. Stortvaer Gade, between Main and Back St. LD $$-$$$*

RESTAURANTS JUST EAST OF CHARLOTTE AMALIE
BANANA TREE GRILL

Legendary St. Thomas restauranteurs Liz and Jerry Buckalew are the masterminds behind this appealing restaurant perched on a high hill with an absolutely stunning view. Tables are on a broad terrace way above Charlotte Amalie and the harbor and are open to the gentle Caribbean breezes. At twilight time and after dark the scene of the twinkling lights below and in the hills is simply magical. In fact, one of the great sights here is seeing a big full moon come popping out from behind the hills of St. Thomas. Dine on garlic-lime mahi mahi, roasted chicken "under a brick," Italian herb- and pancko-seared salmon, lobster tail tempura, or a NY strip Gaetano. Bacon-wrapped shrimp or crab-stuffed mushrooms are tasty starters and the Godiva chocolate brownies are thrilling. Stay for an after-dinner specialty coffee. A cozy little bar is just inside the entrance. *Reservations necessary. Closed Mon. 340.776.4050. Bluebeard's Castle on Bluebeard Hill. D $$-$$$*

HAVANA BLUE

Definitely dine at least once at this ultracool St. Thomas hot spot that overlooks Morningstar Bay. Gauzy white curtains billow in the Caribbean breezes that sweep through huge, open-air windows. The lighting is low and the music has a soft, tropical beat. It's a sexy background for an evening of Cuban/Pacific Rim fusion cuisine. The quietest and most romantic tables hug the edge of the large dining room and showcase ocean views, but take a center table or dine at the bar if you want to feel part of the crowd. Panko-crusted brie or the Latin Trio, with yucca chips to dip into black bean hummus, guacamole, and pica de gallo, are good starting points. Artfully arranged entrees include a sesame-painted grouper with baby bok choy and cipollini onions; an ancho chili- and espresso-rubbed filet; and Polynesian duck. *Reservations necessary. 340.715.2583. Morning Star Beach (at Marriott but privately owned). D $$-$$$*

ROOM WITH A VIEW

French doors frame spectacular views of the harbor and the glittering lights of Charlotte Amalie at this appealing, air-conditioned bistro and wine bar perched on a hillside just above town. Dark hardwood, deep tangerine walls, red carpet, and dim lighting (there's a little lamp on each table) provide a dark and romantic setting. The crab crepe, French onion soup, and brie almondine make good appetizers. For a main course, try the NY strip, lobster Thermidore, Creole shrimp, chicken marsala, or one of the fresh catches of the day. The extensive wine list is reasonably priced and includes an interesting selection of both half and large-format bottles and many wines by the glass. Ice cream sundaes are a specialty and this is a great stop for dessert and an after-dinner drink. *Dinner until midnight. Closed Sun. 340.774.2377. Bluebeard's Castle, Bluebeard Hill. D $$*

FRENCHTOWN RESTAURANTS
ALEXANDER'S BELLA BLU

A superb chef, a classy atmosphere, and a remarkably varied menu make this a great choice. Paintings adorn the sponged gray walls of this stylish, sophisticated, air-conditioned stop with excellently prepared cuisine. Try one of the delicious, authentic schnitzels (wiener, jaeger, or zigeuner) made with veal or chicken. Or select pasta with pesto or marinara or alfredo or meatballs. You can also dine on salmon in an herb crust, tuna with a pink peppercorn sauce, snapper Provencal, a NY strip, or a Caesar, Greek, or spinach salad alone or with shrimp, steak, or lamb chops added. The olive tray, sausage sampler with mustard, and the fried calamari are delightful beginnings. There's a small bar in back. *Reservations necessary for dinner. Closed Sun. 340.774.4349. Frenchtown Mall. LD $$-$$$*

CRAIG AND SALLY'S

Two owners who really care, a great (albeit extremely eclectic) menu, and excellent food served in a casual but cosmopolitan atmosphere make this place worth coming back to again and again. There are seascape murals on the walls, several air-conditioned dining areas, and comfortable low lighting. Craig and Sally love to run a restaurant and it shows. The inspired and lengthy menu changes nightly and bears thorough investigation. One night the filet mignon might be stuffed with Danish blue cheese; the next night it might be served atop garlic-roasted mashed potatoes. You might find slow-braised ossobucco with black bean salsa or prosciutto-wrapped mahi mahi or Atlantic salmon over baby leaf spinach with a warm vinaigrette sauce. Tuna, sea bass, pasta, lamb, veal, duck, beef—you'll find it all, prepared in wonderful ways. Sooner or later you'll notice that crates of wine are stacked here and there all over the place. Craig is the wine connoisseur and offers ones that are truly unusual. Check and see what he's got when you're there. Some wines are real bargains. There's a large, comfortable bar also. *Reservations necessary. Closed Mon.-Tues. No lunch Sat.-Tues. 340.777.9949. Frenchtown. LD $$-$$$*

EPERNAY

Small tables run along one side of this tiny, dark, and sophisticated wine bar and bistro with a classy decor. Hung from the ceiling are green shades, which hover just above the tables, giving off an intimate glow. A few tables are also outside. The menu choices are quite varied. Begin with a warm spinach salad with blue cheese or a classic Caesar or fried calamari with lemon-mayo remoulade. Entrees include chicken stuffed with roasted garlic over capellini and spinach, cassoulet, steak frites, seared salmon with braised fennel, and a shrimp and goat cheese pizza. Or just have one after another of the tempting appetizers: polenta with mushroom ragout, tuna carpaccio, or the Epernay Platter with smoked salmon, brie, and pate. *Closed Sun., no lunch Sat. Dinner until 11 p.m.; Fri., Sat. until midnight. 340.774.5348. Frenchtown Mall. LD $-$$*

HOOK, LINE, AND SINKER

When you are in the mood for a casual coffee shop atmosphere and menu plus outstanding food, this weathered gray spot is the place to come. The decor is on the plain side, with booths along the walls, simple tables, and a counter with stools. Windows open to tropical breezes and you can see pelicans diving for food. This is the kind of place that you could come to seven days in a row and have something different and it would all be good. Burgers are great but so is the chili and the salads and the lunchtime sandwiches. There's a terrific Reuben and also a great Black Russian

MARGARITA PHIL'S

Frenchtown's Margarita Phil's is bordered by two cast iron "faux" cactus and a rustic wooden fence. Directly beyond the fence is a courtyard with tables and an outside bar. If you prefer to chill, head inside to the air-conditioned dining room. Like its sister restaurant in St. John, this place serves truly authentic Mexican cuisine. Come here for superb enchiladas, tacos, fajitas, and quesadillas as well as excellent fresh fish dishes and daily specials. And, of course, the margaritas are exceptional. Crowds gather for the monthly Tequila tastings and the cooking classes fill up fast. Call for dates and times. *340.777.TACO. Frenchtown. LD $$*

OCEANA RESTAURANT & WINE BAR

Come here for true al fresco dining overlooking the water. There are no walls, just a tin roof and a broad terrace and nicely spaced tables. The view looks out to East Gregorie Channel and Water and Hassel Islands. Patricia LaCorte, a famous local chef, has created an eclectic, globally inspired menu. Appetizers include spiced shrimp with mango-melon salsa, Thai-style asparagus soup with fresh lobster, and a tapas platter. Entrees include jumbo diver scallops with shiitake mushrooms, spinach, and roasted garlic; lamb with portobello mushroom and a grilled vegetable and goat cheese potato puree napoleon; and a filet/garlic shrimp combo with Yukon gold potato puree. There's an inside bar and a lounge with pleasant seating inside and out. *340.774.4262. Villa Olga. Sunday Brunch. D $$$*

blackboard at the entrance details the evening's specials. Plastic tables are in a little courtyard hidden by white latticework and decorated with tiny white lights. *Compass Point Marina. No phone. D $-$$*

EAST END RESTAURANTS

AGAVE TERRACE

Dining here is on a little terrace or in a breezy room with open walls. Seafood is the specialty at this popular restaurant, which can be extremely busy, especially on-season. Your server will inform you of the day's choice of catches—four or five fresh fish daily—prepared pan-fried, baked, grilled, blackened, or poached. If you've spent the day on a deep-sea fishing trip, they'll be happy to prepare your catch. The menu also includes grilled steaks, a grilled chicken breast, and a handful of pasta dishes. The view of St. John and the British Virgin Islands from the terrace and the bar is truly spectacular. *Reservations necessary. 340.775.4142. East End on Smith Bay Road at Point Pleasant Resort. D $$*

AZURE

Tucked into the hillside in Sapphire Village is this small and casual eatery. Tables are inside, with windows open to the breezes, and outside on a terrace around a small swimming pool. The food is skillfully prepared. Try the pork egg rolls with a spicy Thai dipping sauce or pernod-flamed escargot or a bowl of PEI mussels to start. Entrees include chicken piccata; grilled steaks; duck breast on stir-fried vegetables with hoisin

MOLLY MOLONE'S

This open-air eatery is extremely casual and very popular with locals, yachties, and vacationers from morning to night. There's a large bar with six TVs and tables are under an awning or outside on a terrace facing a little waterfall. Despite the name, much more than Irish items are on the menu. So drop by for Molly McOmlettes, pancakes, and French toast in the morning. Come back for fish 'n' chips or shepherd's pie or a cheeseburger or a Philly cheese steak or barbecued ribs or a steak. Or just stop by the bar for an icy brew or a frozen island drink. *340.775.1270. American Yacht Harbor, Red Hook. BLD $-$$*

OFF THE HOOK

A long, open hallway leads out to this al fresco restaurant, where casual tables are placed on a broad terrace overlooking the American Yacht Harbor Marina. Locals, tourists, and seafood lovers come here to enjoy the soft ocean breezes and dine on fresh fish. Try the local yellowtail snapper roasted in banana leaves with creole sauce, or blackened mahi mahi with asparagus hash, or seared tuna with wasabi mashed potatoes. There's also a penne with a basil cream sauce and a filet mignon with sauce au poivre. Starters include tuna tartare, fried calamari, jerk chicken skewers, and a conch and seafood callalloo. *Reservations necessary on season. 340.775.6350. Red Hook. D $$-$$$*

ROMANO'S

Don't miss Romano's. This is **the place** on-season and reservations are a must to dine at Tony Romano's swank northern Italian restaurant. Fresh flowers are on the table and the service is professional at this slightly bright, very upscale delight. The menu is classic (and not-so-classic, but equally delicious) northern Italian: ossobucco, veal scallopine marsala, linguine with sweet clams, shrimp with sweet red peppers. Soups of the day might include an outstanding roasted carrot or cauliflower puree. Flourless dark chocolate cake and a poached pear with chocolate sauce are two tempting desserts. Keep an eye out for Tony. A truly dedicated chef, he works hard in the kitchen, but often wanders out toward the end of the evening to greet his guests. This is one of the most popular restaurants on St. Thomas and you may have to wait a bit on-season, even with a reservation. There's a little terrace where you can have a drink but it's far more interesting to sit at the bar and check out the huge number of interesting spirits and grappas that crowd the shelves. Check out the paintings and watercolors adorning the walls. Some are by artists Tony discovers in the Dominican Republic. Others are by Tony himself, who, in addition to being a great chef is also an acclaimed artist. (If you were lucky, you may have caught his one-man show in Manhattan.) Cigar lovers will want to try a Tony Romano smoke, or even take some home in the handsome box. This truly is a restaurant you do not want to miss. *Closed Sun. 340.775.0045. Coral World Rd., Smith Bay. D $$-$$$*

ST. THOMAS RITZ-CARLTON GREAT BAY GRILL

If you are looking for a special place to celebrate an anniversary or wanting a quiet and romantic venue to pop the question, or are just in the mood to dress up, the Great Bay Grill is the perfect destination. It's classic Ritz-Carlton. Tables set with crisp linens and signature blue stemware are in several intimate, air-conditioned dining rooms. The service is predictably gracious and the presentation refined. Perhaps lobster bisque or a shrimp cocktail with papaya mango salsa to begin, followed by baby red snapper baked in a banana leaf or ahi tuna or a filet mignon. The Sunday brunch offers numerous stations of exquisitely arranged delights and an entire room devoted to desserts. *Reservations essential. Closed Mon.-Wed. Brunch only Sun. 340.775.3333. 6900 Great Bay. D $$$*

WHALE OF A TALE

Upstairs, right above Molly Molone's, is this hideaway that is a true favorite with locals. The ceiling is high, the decor is nautical, and the walls are dark wood. Tall French doors invite in the tropical breezes. Those in the know come here for very fresh locally caught fish. Check out the nightly specials. This is also a place to come for clams, Caribbean lobster, and Maryland crab cakes as well as chicken dishes and pasta dishes, including the excellent plum tomato marinara. Frozen bushwacker pie with butterscotch sauce is a tasty choice for dessert. *340.775.1270. American Yacht Harbor, Red Hook. D $$*

NORTH SHORE RESTAURANTS
OLD STONE FARM HOUSE

The setting is magnificent. This beautiful stone house was originally a sugar plantation Great House two centuries ago and it's the perfect setting for an elegant restaurant. Three rooms with hardwood floors are separated by stunning stone walls with broad and gracious archways. The inspired menu is contemporary and creative and quite varied. For appetizers, you might start with Prince Edward Island mussels with housemade chorizo sausage and goat cheese or ahi tuna and pesto tartar. Then you might choose blackened salmon with black bean mango slaw or a malt and honey marinated pork chop. Come early for a beverage in the romantic courtyard complete with fountain. *Reservations necessary. Closed Mon. 340.777.6277. Rte. 42 at Mahogany Run. D $$-$$$*

SOME GREAT BAKERIES, DELIS, AND TAKE-OUT FOOD

Havensight
Cream and Crumbs Shop *(340.774.2499)*, which is in Havensight, features freshly ground coffee, tasty pastries, and rolls.

Frenchtown
Frenchtown Deli *(340.776.7211)* makes great sandwiches (create your own or choose from the list on the board: meatball wedge, reuben, croissant with ham and cheese, etc.) and sells chips and cold sodas and beer. Take it away or walk through to the other side and you'll find tables with books and newspapers scattered about. For breakfast, you can get eggs, bacon, toast and fresh orange juice.

Red Hook
Cold Stone Creamery *(340.777.2777)*, at the American Yacht Harbor, is hard to pass up if you have any interest at all in ice cream, which is made here fresh daily. Flavors can be combined into "Creations"—see the blackboard for a list of the featured combinations of the day, or be creative and choose an exotic combo of your own making. You can get shakes, smoothies, and sundaes, too.

Burrito Bay Deli *(340.775.2944)* makes traditional sandwiches—ham, tuna, roast beef plus burritos and tacos and hot selections and more.

Marina Market *(340.779.2411)* features excellent food to go. Come and choose a delicious salad or order a sandwich or pick up a prepared meal for the whole family.

TAXIS AND TAXI DRIVERS

Taxis in St. Thomas can range from compact cars that hold just a few passengers, to large old station wagons that can accommodate a medium-size family plus luggage, to vans and open-air safari buses that can carry close to 20 people.

It is the custom in St. Thomas, and many other islands, to fill up the taxi with people before heading off. People from the mainland are generally "in a hurry" and can think it's a waste of their vacation time to be made to wait for other people. However, there is another point of view. Consider, for example, that an islander sees not filling the van as a waste of space (empty seats), a waste of fuel (making the trip twice), and lost income. Plus, what's the hurry? You're in the islands! (Private taxis can be arranged, see below.)

TAXI TIPS

❏If you are planning to get a taxi from the airport, you'll discover that this is a good time to begin practicing your adjustment to "island time." You'll find that vans sometimes even "wait for the next plane" (which actually won't be that long, since it is probably already on the ground). Hurrying won't get you to your final destination any sooner, and since you have probably already been traveling (including waiting time) from somewhere between four and 17 hours, what's another 15 minutes? Feel and breathe the air and look around. If you are alone or with one or two others and want to head to your destination immediately, look for a cab that is almost full. But the best thing to do is to go have a beer at the bar near the luggage carousel and then go get in a cab. You'll most likely find your planemates inside, waiting! If you want a private taxi at the airport, just ask. Or call **Chris' Taxi Service** *(340.690.1581)*. The rates are fairly expensive.

❑If you are in Charlotte Amalie and want to go to Havensight, the quickest way is to look for a fairly full van or safari bus where the driver is calling, "Back to the ship." Just hop on and tell the driver you want to go to the Havensight shops.

❑At hotels, taxis wait in line, and the hotel or doorman will fill taxis with people heading to similar destinations. This can be a good way to meet people and share information.

❑Don't be shy about taking the front seat next to the driver of your taxi. He or she will be pleased. Do buckle up. It's the law in St. Thomas, and taken very seriously.

❑If you get a chance, converse with the taxi drivers. They are generally not only kind but very interesting people. Some have lived on St. Thomas for years and can tell you stories about St. Thomas long ago. Many grew up on other Caribbean islands—Tortola in the BVI, St. Kitts, Antigua, Dominica. You'll also find out that many of the drivers have had numerous careers and lived for long periods in Hartford, Connecticut; or New York City; or Omaha.

❑If you call to have a taxi pick you up, you'll be given the number of the taxi that will come to get you. This number is also the taxi license number so it's easy to know if the taxi headed your way is actually "yours."

❑Taxi fares are regulated and the yellow *St. Thomas This Week* prints these fares. The rates in parentheses are for each passenger traveling to the same destination. Keep this list and agree on the fare with the driver before you leave. Some drivers charge for luggage. Most drivers are honest and helpful but a few do try to take advantage. The telephone number for the Taxi Lost and Found is 340.776.8294. *For a list of taxi drivers' phone numbers, see page 139.*

THE OLD AIRPORT

Travelers who first headed to St. Thomas before the early '90s remember a completely different airport—rustic perhaps, but chock full of character, and with a long, long walk to the plane. Those who know both airports might enjoy the following story.

AN ISLAND STORY

We have this friend. He lived in New York, but his heart belonged to the Virgin Islands. Several times a year for over two decades the St. Thomas Airport was the gateway to the islands he loved so much.

Each time he de-planed and made that long walk to the WWII hangar that was the terminal building, he made his first stop in what to him was a very special place.

This place had no resemblance to "Rick's" and was unquestionably the opposite of "A Clean Well-Lighted Place." This place was that weary, dark, stale-smelling Sparky's Airport Bar.

Our friend wasn't even much of a drinker, but through the years a cold Sparky's Heineken became almost sacramental. It was the phone booth where his mind slipped out of its three-piece suit and into an island shirt.

Finally, after years of just visiting, he and the wife he loved so much were actually moving—taking up residence in these beautiful islands. A dream come true, as they say.

The plane landed at dusk and it was very crowded. The man and his wife entered the terminal from a strange direction. Things seemed different in the airport. Our friend was a little disoriented so he snagged a skycap. "Sorry, how would I get to Sparky's from here?" he asked.

"Sparky's finish, mon. This terminal all new. Progress, don't ya know."

Time stopped for a second or two. Then our friend turned to his wife . . . smiled . . . and said, "That's okay. No problem. I wasn't really that thirsty."

He didn't fool her.

— Reprinted from *The Best of the Peter Island Morning Sun*

CHAPTER 3

GREAT ST. THOMAS WINE BARS, QUIET BARS, LIVELY BARS

"'Twas a woman who
drove me to drink,
and I never had
the courtesy
to thank her for it."
— *W.C. Fields*

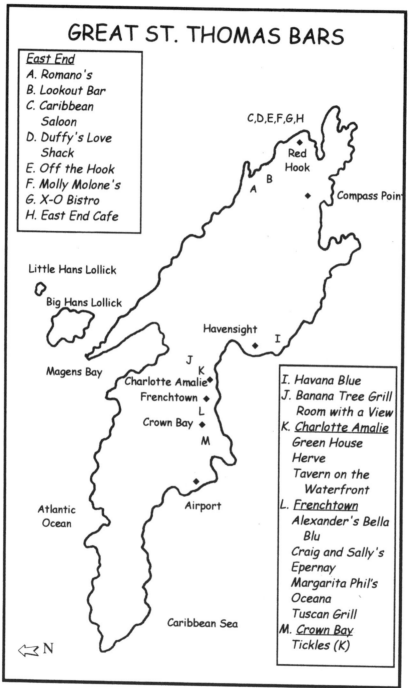

GREAT ST. THOMAS BARS

East End
A. Romano's
B. Lookout Bar
C. Caribbean
   Saloon
D. Duffy's Love
   Shack
E. Off the Hook
F. Molly Molone's
G. X-O Bistro
H. East End Cafe

C,D,E,F,G,H

Red
Hook

A B

Compass Point

Little Hans Lollick

Big Hans Lollick

Havensight

I

J
  K
Charlotte Amalie
   Frenchtown
      L
   Crown Bay
      M

Magens Bay

Atlantic
Ocean

Airport

Caribbean Sea

N

I. Havana Blue
J. Banana Tree Grill
   Room with a View
K. *Charlotte Amalie*
   Green House
   Herve
   Tavern on the
      Waterfront
L. *Frenchtown*
   Alexander's Bella
      Blu
   Craig and Sally's
   Epernay
   Margarita Phil's
   Oceana
   Tuscan Grill
M. *Crown Bay*
   Tickles (K)

OCEANA RESTAURANT AND WINE BAR

Inside, settle into a love seat or belly up to the comfortable bar or head to a table outside along the narrow terrace and enjoy the soft sea breezes. This could be the time to try a real island drink, like a frozen strawberry margarita or their house specialty, the pomegranate flirtini. *340.774.4262.*

TICKLES DOCKSIDE PUB

It's not really in Frenchtown, but actually the next bay west, at Crown Bay Marina, which is also where you catch the ferry to Water Island (the dock is next to the restaurant). This is a great open-air bar with wonderful views of water and boats and good casual fare: burgers and fries, chili with cheese, conch chowder, BBQ pork. Locals flock here morning to night and for the always popular happy hour. *340.776.1595. Crown Bay Marina.*

TUSCAN GRILL

This is a small restaurant and the bar is quiet but comfortable. You can dine at the bar if you want (*see menu page 37*). *Closed Sun. 340.776.4211.*

EAST END BARS

CARIBBEAN SALOON

The bar is big and busy and popular with young and old alike. In fact many of the bartenders and wait staff that work at this end of the island hang here at the end of their day (often the wee morning hours) and the menu of burgers, wings, fried calamari, and meatball subs is served from 11 a.m. to 4 a.m. *340.775.7060. American Yacht Harbor. Red Hook.*

DUFFY'S LOVE SHACK

The draw at this casual, funky establishment is the mix of icy cold beers, tasty frozen drinks, lots of people, and rock and roll music turned up high. They serve food here, too. *340.779.2080. Red Hook.*

EAST END CAFE

If you're seeking air-conditioning, romantic lighting, and a long and elegant bar, then this might be your destination. Belly up for a glass of wine, a single malt, or an island special. *340.715.1442. Red Hook.*

LOOKOUT BAR

The seats here provide one of the very best views of St. John and the nearby British Virgin Islands. The sun sets in the opposite direction but sunsets are still striking here. To avoid the crowds waiting for dinner at the popular adjoining Agave Terrace restaurant, walk past the bar to the tiny outside terrace. *340.775.4142. Point Pleasant Resort, Smith Bay Rd.*

MOLLY MOLONE'S

Belly up to the bar at this popular stop, have an icy-cold beer and catch the latest sports on one of the six TVs or swap stories with yachties, locals, and vacationers. *340.775.1270. American Yacht Harbor.*

OFF THE HOOK

The bar is open-air and looks out to the marina and the many boats at dock and is popular with locals. *340.775.6350. Red Hook.*

ROMANO'S

This narrow little bar has comfortable seats and you can spend an hour or two reading the labels on all the bottles of grappa and other interesting spirits and wines that line the wall. Or look the other way and gaze at the wonderful paintings on the walls, some collected by the owner who searches out aspiring artists in the Dominican Republic, and some painted by chef/owner Tony Romano, who happens to be an acclaimed artist as well as an award-winning chef. The art is for sale, if something happens to catch your eye. *Closed Sun. 340.775.0045. Smith Bay Rd.*

X-O BISTRO

Champagnes and wines by the glass plus a full bar are the draw at this late-night watering hole. There's also a menu and you can dine at the bar or one of the little tables. Snack on shrimp escargot, share a cheese board for two or a pizza or try one of the heartier nightly specials, such as pork ribs over garlic mashed potatoes or lamb shank over blue cheese polenta. *340.779.2069. Red Hook.*

A BEVERAGE UNDER THE STARS

This chapter suggests almost two dozen different venues to enjoy a margarita or martini, a frozen daiquiri or a diet coke. Wonderful choices for a pre-dinner cocktail, a glass of wine, or an after-dinner eau de vie...but one really great choice is missing from the preceding list. That choice is the deck, balcony, terrace, or beach right outside the door to the room or villa where you are staying.

It's peaceful and private. And whether you choose to watch the day melt into evening with a cocktail before dinner or return from dinner and sit sipping under the stars, the experience is one that should definitely not be missed.

ALWAYS . . .

Always be nicer to people than necessary.

Always lock your hotel room and rental car.

Always have a hat, bandanna, or something to cover your head during the day.

Always remember to keep left when you are driving.

Always look right first, and then left before crossing the street.

Always put on some sunscreen before going outside during the day.

Always greet people and ask how they are doing before conducting any "business."

Always remember the sometimes slower pace you encounter is part of the island charm.

Always snorkel with at least one other person.

ST. CROIX

FOR THE DAY

St. Croix sits by itself about 40 miles south of St. Thomas so it takes a bit longer to get there than it does to get to most of the other neighboring islands. However, you'll still have enough time to have fun on St. Croix, provided you have something specific in mind—you won't have time to do everything.

You can drive around the island and visit several beaches. **Olympic Car Rental** *rents cars near the dock (340.772.2000), or you can take yourself on a historic walk through downtown Christiansted (directions in the free* St. Croix This Week*).*

You can grab a tour boat to the Buck Island Reef National Monument (which is different from the Buck Island just off St. Thomas), or you can ride through a rain forest on horseback. Call **Paul and Jill's Equestrian Stables** *(340.772.2880).*

How can you get there? You can take a regular plane or a seaplane or even a ferry. However, please check to see what is running when you are on island. Over the last 15 years plane schedules, seaplane service, and boat transportation between the islands of St. Thomas and St. Croix has changed often (and several hydrofoils have come and gone).

BY PLANE

It's a 20- to 30-minute flight and planes leave from the St. Thomas airport. **Cape Air** *(800.352.0714)* flies between St. Thomas and St. Croix several times daily. Round-trip, same-day fare is $133.50. Book early, as these flights can fill up fast.

BY SEAPLANE

A neat seaplane flies from the Charlotte Amalie Waterfront (at the Marine Terminal, where the ferries leave for the BVI) to right in front of the Best Western hotel in Christiansted. It's a quick 17 minutes in the air. There are several morning flights and, for day-trippers, a convenient afternoon return. Fare is $164–$168. Call **Seaborne Seaplanes** *(340.773.6442)*.

BY FERRY

It takes about an hour and 15 minutes to travel by ferry between St. Thomas and St. Croix and the fares and schedules change often. Call **Boston Harbor Cruises Ferry** *(877.733.9425)*, which operates a ferry service from November to May. The fare is $70 round trip. Also **Island Lynx Ferry Service** *(340.773.9500)* offers service between St. Thomas and St. Croix. **Virgin Islands Fast Ferry** *(340.719.0099)* operates daily except Tuesday from mid-December through the end of April. The fare is $77 round trip. Bear in mind that this ride can be rough if the seas are up.

SNORKELING HINTS FOR BEGINNERS

❑ When it is sunny, you'll find that you will see more and it will be clearer if you snorkel between 8 a.m. to 10 a.m.

❑ Protect the reefs. Coral is extremely fragile and it grows very slowly. Never touch it, never step on it with your flippers, and never anchor your boat in coral.

❑ Watch out for black blobs with spikes nestled in the rocks. These are sea urchins and they sting. The bigger they are, the worse the pain.

❑ Parrot fish make their own little sleeping bags each night. If you spot things that look like little plastic sacs, it could be sleeping fish.

❑ Speaking of parrot fish, they are big beach builders. They and other reef fish eat algae that grow on coral and inadvertently also take in bits of the coral skeletons, which they later excrete as sand!

❑ If you want to dive a bit deeper than you can comfortably snorkel, but don't want tanks on your back, try **Snuba**. The air tank remains on a float above the water and follows you around. *Reservations necessary. Mon.-Sat. 11 a.m. and 1 p.m., Sun. 1 p.m. $57. Trunk Bay. 340.693.8063.*

CHARLOTTE AMALIE SHOPPING
(Havensight, Red Hook shops, and Tillet Gardens appear at the end of this chapter.)

Everyone knows that Charlotte Amalie is a world-class duty-free shopping mecca, but what no one ever points out is that there are also wonderful, original shops—intriguing stores even for people who hate to shop—with items you may never find anywhere else tucked here and there in the Charlotte Amalie alleyways.

Charlotte Amalie certainly gets its share of negative comments. People complain that it's too crowded and full of street hawkers. Well, there are hawkers and it can be very crowded when many cruise ships are in. Also, the town is somewhat confusing, and this is compounded by the throngs of people who make it difficult to see where you are.

For some, the crowds are part of the fun. But if you want to avoid them, head downtown mid-afternoon. Many cruise ship shoppers will have returned to their ship and the town can be quite pleasant. It also helps to go when few ships are in (see schedules in St. Thomas This Week). *Some days off-season no ships are in and town is a delight.*

HOW CHARLOTTE AMALIE IS ORGANIZED
Two main streets are parallel to each other and lined with shops: Waterfront Highway (which runs along the harbor) and Main Street. Numerous narrow alleyways, also lined with shops, connect these two streets. Each alleyway has a name (often Danish, with letter combinations non-Danish speaking people can find difficult to pronounce). However, you don't really need to know these names because, although you will see these names on maps, a good number of alleys do not have identifying signs anyway.

FINDING YOUR WAY AROUND
So, how do you find anything in this bit warren of alleyways with nonpronounceable names that often aren't posted? Easy. People rely on landmarks—just about everything is either near the Post Office, or Vendors' Plaza, or First Bank. Don't be embarrassed if you can't find the store you were just in. Even locals get confused. See the map on page 65 to locate easily the shops you want to find.

CHARLOTTE AMALIE SHOPS

The stores below are selected because they have something special to offer. Most aren't famous and some are places that very few people know about. Most will happily ship home whatever you buy. The stores are organized alphabetically by category. Use the numbers next to each shop name to locate it on the map on page 65.

Charlotte Amalie's great duty-free stores—Columbian Emeralds, Royal Caribbean, A.H Riise, Cardow's, Little Switzerland (the stores that sell gemstones, crystal, linens, watches, electronics, perfumes, cosmetics, and liquor)—aren't included below because these renowned shops are covered so thoroughly in free tourist information guides like the yellow St. Thomas This Week *and because you can't miss these large shops. If you are hoping to get a good deal on a specific item, be sure you know the stateside price of the exact same item (same model number, size, number of features, etc.).*

ANTIQUES

CARSON CO. ANTIQUES (18)

Old brick archways provide a tasteful background for these two rooms of antiquities from ancient times through the 19th century. Come to this well-organized shop for old books (some rare), ancient coins, maps, pottery, African masks, estate and ancient jewelry, and a huge stock of Christmas ornaments. *340.774.6175. Northwest end of Royal Dane Mall W.*

S.O.S (20)

This is a wonderful shop to explore. The specialty is registered ancient coins from all over the world but the owners also run a salvage shop which is the source of much of what you see. The walls are hung with artwork and old maps of the Caribbean and antique parts of boats are on display and for sale. There are beautiful ship wheels and lanterns, plus old coins (some in pins, pendants, and rings), maps, books on the Caribbean, and even old USVI license plates. A brilliantly colored parrot speaks her mind. *340.774.2074. On Waterfront Hwy. at Royal Dane Mall West.*

ART AND GIFT ITEMS

INTO THE SEA (15)

Shelves here are chock-full of delights: handcrafted pottery by Bamboushay of Tortola, Virgin Island soaps and body lotions, beach bags, handbags, wind chimes, watercolors, locally made necklaces and bracelets, batik sarongs. It's a small shop but you'll find a wide selection of Caribbean-made arts and crafts. *340.779.1280. Royal Dane Mall.*

...showcases the art of Mitch Gibbs. He works in ...rcolor, pastel, and acrylic and has several distinctive styles, all appealing. Look for incredibly realistic paintings of Caribbean islands, water, waves, sunsets, and clouds. *No phone. North end of Palm Passage.*

PANGBORN COLLECTION (22)

This is a shop designed for casual browsing. Artful displays along the wall and on well-spaced tables feature incense and candles, espresso cups and coffee mugs, men's ties, decorated champagne glasses, unique clocks, body lotions and soaps, pottery, and even magnets and note cards with amusing quotes. *340.775.4343. Center of Palm Passage.*

SUN FEATHER BATH & BEAUTY(12)

Design your own personal soap here and then watch it be made. Just select your original blend of luxurious oils, butters, fragrances, botanicals, and natural pigments. You can also shop here for candles, ready-made unique soaps, bath oils, sea sponges, and delightful gift baskets. *340.775.2466. Near Main Street on Trompeter Gade.*

TOUBA HOMELAND (28)

For authentic handcrafted African and Caribbean clothing, artwork, crafts, and reggae items, nothing beats this tiny shop. Look for African rattles, handwoven satchels, dainty earrings, wood and stone carvings, genuine African dresses and tunics in handsome fabrics and shades, ceremonial masks, colorful cotton belts, and charming dolls. *340.774.2868. Inside (on the west side) of International Plaza.*

watercolors ...

books on the Caribbean, ...

poster tubes for easy traveling. This is a popular spot and also
cramped, but definitely worth the stop, so if it's too crowded for you,
come back later in the day. *340.776.2303, ext. 141. Entrance on Main St.,
in the middle of the A. H. Riise Walkway.*

DOWN ISLAND TRADERS (4)

There is much more to this store than the T-shirts and Caribbean teas,
coffees, spices, and jams just inside the entrance. Look for a delightful
potpourri of island wares—hand-painted Christmas tree ornaments,
pottery from the St. Thomas Kilnworks, island artwork, watercolor maps
of the Caribbean, cards and watercolors by Flukes of the British Virgin
Islands, teas and coffees, greeting cards and cookbooks, beach bags, beach
towels, island music, and sterling silver jewelry. *340.776.4641. East end
of Waterfront Hwy. shops, just west of Vendors' Plaza.*

CLOTHING (CASUAL)

LOCAL COLOR (13)

This is a great place to come for comfortable sundresses and shirts and
casual pants and capris in bright island prints. Jams, Fresh Produce, Sloop
Jones, Spirit, and Flax lines of clothing are featured. There are some shorts
and shirts for men and plenty of items for kids. *340.774.2280. On
Waterfront Hwy. at corner of Royal Dane Mall East.*

FRESH PRODUCE (8)

Bright pastels and comfort are the hallmarks of this popular line of
clothing. You'll find a huge selection of pants, tops, bathing suits, and
sundresses for women, as well as a children's section, and a smaller

outfits for women are displayed just inside the entrance. Head deeper into the store if you are looking for Jams, Axis, Island Paradise, Nat Nash, and other well-known brands. *340.774.7580. On Waterfront Hwy. at corner of Palm Passage.*

CLOTHING (DESIGNER)

CUCKOO'S NEST (29)

A good selection of men's slacks, sport jackets, suspenders, shoes, silk T-shirts, and button-down shirts are offered here at excellent prices. There are also jackets, suits, and dresses for women. *340.776.4005. Walk from Waterfront Hwy. deep into International Plaza.*

NICOLE MILLER BOUTIQUE (26)

Nicole Miller became famous for her absolutely stunning, delightfully whimsical ties and now, of course, she fashions all manner of things out of these amusing silk prints. They're all available here—umbrellas, dop kits, address books, boxer shorts, swimsuits, bathrobes, vests, jackets, shirts, and ties. Stop here also for Ms. Miller's line of very sexy, feminine clothing—in solids as well as her famous prints. The 1,300-square-foot boutique with white marble floors is a cool classy venue to show off these sensational silk designs. The exceptionally courteous and knowledgeable staff will help you find what you are looking for. *340.774.8286. On Main St. at Palm Passage.*

PALMSIDE (23)

Stop in here for fabulous and truly unique clothes for women: flashy shoes, sequined dresses, and chic purses and belts. Don't leave without selecting at least one pair of great sunglasses from the wall display! *340.715.1202. In Palm Passage near Waterfront Hwy.*

POLO RALPH LAUREN ESQUIRE SHOP (25)

Floor-to-ceiling shelves display rows and rows of neatly folded cable sweaters and knit shirts. Rows of long pants, shorts, and bathing suits hang against the wall. And tables display socks, belts, and nicely arranged stacks of colorful clothing. Most of the items are for men but there is a small selection of sportswear for women and some La Coste items designed for kids. *340.774.8018. Near Main St. in Palm Passage.*

TOMMY HILFIGER OUTLET (11)

Tommy Hilfiger fans will want to head into this huge store, which has a bit of everything for the whole family, all branded with his famous moniker, and marked down in price. You can find some really great deals here. *340.777.1189. On Waterfront Hwy. between Royal Dane Mall and Trompeter Gade.*

DRUGSTORE

OTC DRUGSTORE (9)

If you've run out of your favorite shampoo or need shaving cream or aspirin or a stateside magazine, just walk right through Mr. Tablecloth and up several steps. *340.774.5432. Corner of Main St. and Nye Gade.*

JEWELRY AND SCULPTURES

OKIDANOKH GOLDCRAFT (17)

Arched doorways, brick walls, and fanciful illustrations of unicorns and hot-air balloons create a peaceful setting for display tables showcasing finely handcrafted gold and silver jewelry. Look for delicate and very original earrings, necklaces, rings, bracelets, and pendants. *340.774.9677. Back of Royal Dane Mall.*

BERNARD K. PASSMAN GALLERY (6)

This is a remarkable store and gallery showcasing exquisite pieces of jewelry and delicate small black coral sculptures by world-famous Bernard Passman: a miniature piano with all 88 keys ($22,000); a drum set complete with cymbals and several miniature drums—look for the swirls on the drums, which are the natural swirls in the coral ($28,000); a delicate image of a can-can girl with 22–karat gold boots ($175,000). Perhaps the most famous is that of Charlie Chaplin, with his dog—in solid gold—next to him. It's been valued at $1.2 million. So, what can a regular person afford? Beautiful gold and black coral bracelets, striking diamond and black coral rings, and lovely pendants in the shape of fish with gold eyes. Prices start at $60 and every single piece is exquisitely detailed and initialed. The sales people treat the place as an art gallery and will happily explain the histories behind the more famous pieces even if you are just a browser. *340.777.4580. On Main St., one block west of the Post Office.*

SHOES AND SANDALS

SHOE TREE (5)

This is an excellent spot for brand-name ladies' shoes. You'll find a good selection of sandals, comfortable flats, and dressy heels. Check out the sale shoes on the floor by the cash register. There's almost always at least one great bargain. *340.774.3900. On Cardow's Walk, just beyond the entrance to Bumpa's Cafe.*

ZORA'S (1)

Zora's has been here since 1962 and people come from all over the world for custom-made leather sandals that are exquisitely comfortable and last close to forever. There are also ready-made sandals, canvas bags, famous limin' shoes, Great Wall of China backpacks, kids' canvas shark and fish purses, belly bags, and very cool bottle bags (check out the champagne, tequila, and wine sharks in particular!). If you want custom-made sandals, it takes five days so head here on your first or second day of vacation to get measured and to choose a style (there are at least 50, named after nifty places on nearby islands, like Joe's Hill on Tortola). Before you head home you can stop in for a final fitting and to get your sandals. Zora, her daughters, and Ann are caring craftspeople. When you get home and wish you'd bought that neat cat bag, or want to order another pair of limin' shoes, or decide you want to do all your Christmas shopping at Zora's, just go to www.zora-vi.com. *340.774.2559. From the Post Office walk east on Main St. Go over the little hill and look for the stoplight in the distance. The store is on the right, just before the stoplight.*

SWIM AND BEACH WEAR
DEL SOL (2, 10)
Stuff may look a bit dull inside this shop but take anything here into the sun and then watch out! Like magic, black and white or blue and white designs on T-shirts, beach bags, beach towels, swim trunks, and more transform into a riot of color! And there's more. Nail polish switches from one vivid shade to another. Sunglasses completely change shades. Markers (the kind you draw with) go from one color to another. It's so cool! *340.774.2753. Two locations: Tolbad Gade, across from the Post Office; Waterfront Hwy. between Drake's Passage and Raadets Gade.*

CARIBBEAN SURF COMPANY (14)
If you can use it near water, you'll probably find what you need in this little shop for sunning and beach needs, from sunglasses to sandals, reef shoes, visor hats, bathing suits, swim trunks, and T-shirts. *340.774.1510. Waterfront at Royal Dane Mall East.*

VISITORS' HOSPITALITY LOUNGE
VISITORS' HOSPITALITY LOUNGE (3)
Many visitors don't know that there is a wonderful hospitality lounge run by volunteers that is just for you! Use the restroom, browse through brochures on what to do and where to go, check out the display of local artwork and crafts. You can even leave your luggage here (there's a small charge per piece). And please leave a donation. *340.777.1153. On the corner of Waterfront Hwy. and Tolbad Gade, across from Vendors' Plaza.*

FOR A MAP SHOWING THE LOCATION OF SHOPS DESCRIBED HERE, JUST TURN THE PAGE.

SHOPS IN CHARLOTTE AMALIE
SEE MAP FOR LOCATION

ANTIQUES
Carson Co. Antiques (18)
S.O.S. (20)

ART AND GIFT ITEMS
Into the Sea (15)
Mermaid Cove (16)
Mitch Gibbs (24)
Pangborn Collection (22)
Sun Feather Bath & Beauty (12)
Touba Homeland (28)

BREWERY
Virgin Islands Brewing Co. (19, 27)

CARIBBEAN ITEMS
A. H. Riise Art Gallery (7)
Down Island Traders (4)

CLOTHING (CASUAL)
Local Color (13)
Fresh Produce (8)
Quiet Storm (21)

CLOTHING (DESIGNER)
Cuckoo's Nest (29)
Nicole Miller Boutique (26)
Palmside (23)
Polo Ralph Lauren Esquire (25)
Tommy Hilfiger Outlet (11)

DRUGSTORE
OTC (9)

JEWELRY AND SCULPTURES
Okidanokh Goldcraft (17)
Bernard K. Passman Gallery (6)

SHOES AND SANDALS
Shoe Tree (5)
Zora's (1)

SWIM AND BEACH WEAR
Del Sol (2, 10)
Caribbean Surf Company (14)

**VISITORS'
HOSPITALITY LOUNGE (3)**

1. Zora's
2. Del Sol
3. Visitors Lounge
4. Down Island Traders
5. Shoe Tree
6. Bernard K. Passman
7. A. H. Riise Art Gallery
8. Fresh Produce
9. OTC
10. Del Sol
11. Tommy Hilfiger
12. Sun Feather Bath & Beauty
13. Local Color
14. Caribbean Surf Company
15. Into the Sea
16. Mermaid Cove
17. Okidanokh Goldcraft
18. Carson Co. Antiques
19. Virgin Islands Brewing Company
20. S.O.S.
21. Quiet Storm
22. Pangborn
23. Palmside
24. Mitch Gibbs
25. Polo Esquire Shop
26. Nicole Miller
27. Virgin Islands Brewing Company
28. Touba Homeland
29. Cuckoo's Nest

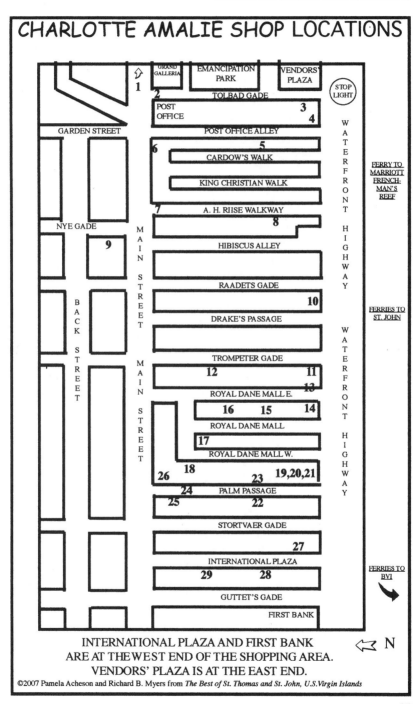

CHARLOTTE AMALIE SHOP LOCATIONS

GRAND GALLERIA
1

EMANCIPATION PARK

VENDORS' PLAZA

STOP LIGHT

2
TOLBAD GADE

POST OFFICE
3
4

GARDEN STREET

POST OFFICE ALLEY

WATERFRONT HIGHWAY

FERRY TO MARRIOTT FRENCH-MAN'S REEF

6
5
CARDOW'S WALK

KING CHRISTIAN WALK

NYE GADE

7
A. H. RIISE WALKWAY
8

MAIN STREET

9

HIBISCUS ALLEY

RAADETS GADE
10

BACK STREET

DRAKE'S PASSAGE

WATERFRONT HIGHWAY

MAIN STREET

TROMPETER GADE
12   11
13

ROYAL DANE MALL E.
16   15   14

ROYAL DANE MALL
17

ROYAL DANE MALL W.

18
26   23   19,20,21
24
PALM PASSAGE
25   22

STORTVAER GADE
27

INTERNATIONAL PLAZA
29   28

GUTTET'S GADE

FIRST BANK

FERRIES TO ST. JOHN

FERRIES TO BVI

INTERNATIONAL PLAZA AND FIRST BANK
ARE AT THE WEST END OF THE SHOPPING AREA.
VENDORS' PLAZA IS AT THE EAST END.

N

©2007 Pamela Acheson and Richard B. Myers from *The Best of St. Thomas and St. John, U.S. Virgin Islands*

HAVENSIGHT SHOPPING

Havensight was built to make it easy for cruise ship passengers to shop without having to go anywhere. Original shops and small branches of many of the duty-free Charlotte Amalie stores are located here in long one-story buildings that stretch back from the cruise ship dock. Also here is the red-roofed Ports of Sale complex. Havensight is never really that crowded and this is an easy place to check out duty-free bargains whether or not you are on a cruise ship and if you don't want to go to town. Many of these shops will be closed if no ships are in.

DOCKSIDE BOOKSHOP
For a superb selection of books in the best bookstore in the Virgin Islands, head straight here. You'll find two floors loaded with hard- and softcover best-sellers, shelves and shelves of novels, mysteries, and adventures, plus books on travel, hobbies, cookbooks, and more. Check out the shelf to the right of the cash register for wonderful books on St. Thomas, the Virgin Islands, and the whole Caribbean. *340.774.4937. Havensight Mall.*

MODERN MUSIC
Across the street from Havensight is this great tape and CD store. Come here for the latest stateside releases plus loads of island music, including albums by Bankie Banx, a terrific recording star from Anguilla. *340.774.3100. Across the street from Havensight's main entrance.*

ELEGANT RESORT SHOPPING
Almost all the larger resorts on St. Thomas and St. John have their own resort shop. (Caneel Bay's, page 125, is one of the best.) And many of the full service resorts like Frenchman's Reef on St. Thomas and The Westin on St. John actually have several shops on property. What this means is that these resort shops may be worth a visit even if you are not staying there, or if you are staying at a larger resort you may not have to leave to do your shopping.

RED HOOK SHOPPING

Red Hook is located at the east end of St. Thomas. If you are staying on this end of the island, or if you are planning to catch the Red Hook ferry to St. John, you might want to check out one or all of these interesting Red Hook shops. All are on the first floor of the American Yacht Harbor complex.

CAPTAIN NAUTICA SURFWEAR HUT
Oneil and Hurley bathing suits, reef walkers, surfing wear, sandals, and skin care creams make this the perfect stop for the whole family before heading to the beach or out on the waves. Also, sign up here for terrific trips to the BVI! *340.715.3379.*

DOLPHIN DREAMS BOUTIQUE
The display windows of this appealing shop are sure to catch your eye. The entrance is actually around the corner. Stop here for hand-painted glassware, island music CDs, books, prints by local artists, handmade soaps, colorful pottery, purses, casual shirts and pants for men and women, gauzy island dresses, and numerous other items. *340.775.0549.*

ELIZABETH JANES
In this enticing jewelry and clothing boutique, lovely silver bracelets and necklaces and earrings are displayed. Need something to wear with your new bracelet? Check out the delightful sandals and handbags and collection of resort clothing. This is also a place to buy the famous Crucian Hook bracelet that is made in St. Croix as well as Crucian Hook earrings and rings. *340.779.1595.*

KEEP LEFT
Stop here for a huge array of island, resort, and warm weather wear for the whole family. You don't necessarily have to keep left, but do keep walking. There's lots to see in this large shop. Look for dresses and capri pants and shirts by Jams. You'll find shorts, bathing suits, shirts, and shoes by Patagonia and Quicksilver. *340.775.9964.*

RHIANNON'S
Glittery and magical fairy dust that you can scatter about for good luck is just one of the delightful things you will find in this New Age store. Tables display spell boxes, good quality incense sticks, a huge array of candles, wonderful books of all sizes, and so much more. There are also delicate earrings, bracelets, and necklaces. If you'd like a tarot reading, just make an appointment. *340.779.1877.*

A VISIT TO TILLET GARDENS

Tillet Gardens is like an oasis within an oasis. Stone walkways, topped by a canopy of spreading shade trees, meander through a peaceful collection of tropical gardens, art galleries, working studios, and small shops.

You can visit **Ridvan Studio** *(340.776.0901)* or **Alison's Wonderland Studio** *(340.998.2470)* and see clay artworks being created or purchase beautiful sconces, wall plaques, or plates and platters and vases.

Or you might want to stop by **The Hand Painted Company** *(340.715.4024)* and pick up a hand-painted beach cover-up or order a personalized hand-painted shirt or hat or piece of pottery. At **Caribbean Herbal and Candles** *(340.777.7190)* you can watch candles and soaps being poured by hand and buy some of them to take a scent of the islands back home.

If a day at a spa is what you're looking for, head to the **Zen Retreat** *(340.774.8044)* for massages, facials, yoga instruction and much more.

The famous **Pistarkle Theatre** *(340.775.7877)* makes its home in Tillet Gardens. The theatre showcases a variety of wonderful entertainment. Call for a schedule.

At **Jack's Restaurant** *(340.776.9464)* treat yourself to a chicken wrap, a great salad, some wings, or their famous and very delicious bison burger.

For more information or directions call 340.775.1929 or log onto www.tilletgardens.com

GREAT THINGS
TO LOOK FOR

THE BIRDS YOU WERE FEEDING LAST SUMMER

If you're here in winter, don't be surprised if some of the birds you see look a lot like the songbirds you had in your backyard last summer. They head here from northern climes every winter, too. Some actually go all the way to South America, stopping here on the way down and on the way back north.

HITCHHIKING BIRDS

If you take a ferry anywhere, look to see if a bird seems to "hang in the air" close to the boat. It'll be a Brown Booby, hitching a ride. You'll see them actually search out a power boat so they can catch a ride in the boat's air wake. If they spot a fish, they'll swoop right down and catch it and then race like crazy to catch back up to the boat to continue their "extra-easy" ride.

HOMEMADE FREIGHTERS

Head down to the Charlotte Amalie waterfront and walk along the harbor until you see some small (and sometimes very simple) cargo boats. Stop and read the handmade signs in front of some of the vessels: "Will take cargo to Dominica, Guadaloupe, and St. Lucia" or "Leaving for Sint Maarten tonight." These small boats travel about from island to island, often carrying bananas or other produce north to St. Thomas and bringing much-needed freight back to some of the southern Caribbean islands.

LOCAL KNOWLEDGE

PERFUME DEALS
You can get great deals on cosmetics and perfumes not only while you are on St. Thomas, but even after you return home. Simply call **A. H. Riise** at 800.524.2037 and place your order.

RECYCLED BALLAST
Many of the bricks used in the buildings on St. Thomas were originally used simply as ballast on the ships that came to St. Thomas to pick up cargo. These ships dumped the bricks and filled their hulls with rum and sugar and returned to Europe.

GETTING LOST
Don't feel stupid if you can't find the store you were in five minutes ago when you are shopping in Charlotte Amalie. This happens to everyone—including people who have lived on St. Thomas for years.

OPENING DAYS
Some restaurants are closed on Sundays . . . several on Mondays, and a few on Tuesdays. But also the days may change at different times of the year. It's probably best to call first on these days or nights.

DOMINOS
You can play dominos or whist every Wednesday and Saturday night at **Percy's Bus Stop.** If you're interested, call Percy at 340.774.5993.

CHAPTER 5

GREAT CHARLOTTE AMALIE LUNCH BREAKS

"Ask not what you can do for your country.
Ask what's for lunch."

—*Orson Welles*

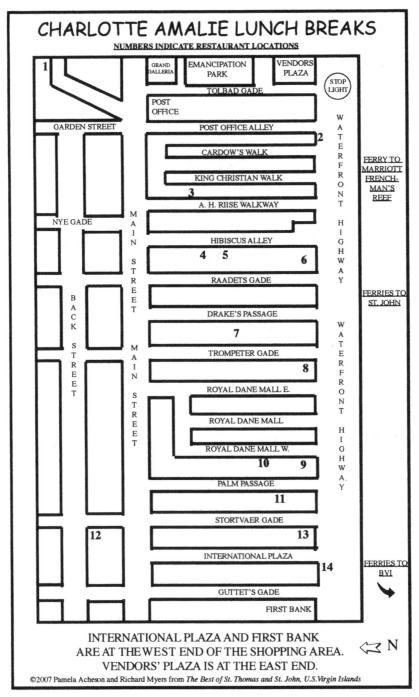

CHARLOTTE AMALIE LUNCH BREAKS

NUMBERS INDICATE RESTAURANT LOCATIONS

INTERNATIONAL PLAZA AND FIRST BANK
ARE AT THE WEST END OF THE SHOPPING AREA.
VENDORS' PLAZA IS AT THE EAST END.

©2007 Pamela Acheson and Richard Myers from *The Best of St. Thomas and St. John, U.S. Virgin Islands*

R & J'S ISLAND LATTE (6)

Relax in air-conditioned comfort with a frozen green tea, or a flavored coffee. Try a little loaf of zucchini bread, or ham and cheese croissant. Sandwiches, breads and muffins, and an extensive coffee and tea menu are the draw here. *340.777.8100. Waterfront Hwy. at Raadets Gade. BL $*

TACO FIESTA (5)

Inside this tiny restaurant you'll find pink walls and white tablecloths and air-conditioning. Tables are outside, too. The cuisine is mainly authentic Mexican, such as tacos, quesadillas, and nachos but there are burgers and salads, too. At breakfast dine on huevos rancheros, a breakfast burrito, or bacon and eggs. *340.774.6600. Midway into Hibiscus Alley. BLD $*

TAVERN ON THE WATERFRONT (8)

Tables line the windows at this air-conditioned, upstairs eatery overlooking the harbor. The varied lunch menu includes a Thai chicken peanut wrap, Polish pierogi, plus burgers, soups, salads, and sandwiches. *Closed Sun. 340.776.4328. Waterfront Hwy. at Royal Dane Mall. LD $-$$*

VIRGILIO'S (12)

When you want an elegant lunch and some of the best Italian food anywhere, come here. Soft lighting and polished service provide the perfect backdrop for a glass of pinot grigio, a salad, and freshly grilled fish or the pasta of the day. Although Virgin Island power lunches are held here, Virgilio's is really meant for lingering and it's a fine place for a long and leisurely lunch. *340.776.4920. Main St. at Stortvaer Gade. LD $$-$$$*

SNACKS AND ICE CREAM
ICE CREAM SHOPPE (14)

This tiny take-away place has delicious ice cream cones, yogurt, and hot dogs, plus West Indian snacks like fish fry, johnnie cakes, chicken soup, and meat pates. *340.776.1621. Waterfront Hwy. at International Plaza.*

If you like chili and happen to be in St. Thomas in late summer or early fall, check with the Texas Society of the Virgin Islands and see if you're lucky enough to be on island during their annual Chili Cookoff. It's one of the island's great happenings!

Several thousand people show up for this all-day event. The Chili Judges (chili connoisseurs, naturally) rate chili samples for aroma, color, and consistency and take into consideration both the immediate taste and the equally important aftertaste.

Once the judges have had their fill, the general public is welcome to sample as many chili offerings as they can, for a quarter each.

The Chili Cookoff is usually held on a beach (which beach varies year to year). There's live music all day long, and there are all kinds of games and contests—tug-o-war and melon seed-spitting, to name just two—and a bunch of prizes. It's a great event and a lot of fun, and money raised goes to local charities.

Call 340.775.8011 or 340.776.3595 if you want to attend or enter your own special chili recipe.

ST. JOHN FOR THE EVENING

Many visitors to St. Thomas never realize how incredibly easy it is to head over to St. John just for dinner. In fact, if you are staying on the east end of St. Thomas, it is possible to go to St. John for dinner in about the same length of time that it would take you to get to downtown Charlotte Amalie. Most of the ferries have an uncovered upper level and you can ride over basking in the afternoon sun and return at night in a seat open to the soft Caribbean breezes and under a blanket of stars and perhaps a full moon.

Getting to and from St. John

The ferry dock is right in the middle of the east end of St. Thomas, at Red Hook. Ferries run hourly on the half hour from 8 a.m. to midnight from Red Hook to Cruz Bay on St. John and the ride takes less than 20 minutes. Get there a little early if you want to be sure to get a seat up top. The fare is $5 and the ferry takes you to the dock right in the heart of Cruz Bay, which is St. John's only real town and very different from anything on St. Thomas. If you prefer a private ride, **Dohm Water Taxi** *(340.775.6501)* will take you over to St. John in one of their wave-piercing power catamarans in a quick 15 minutes and bring you back after dinner. It's $25 per person (minimum of six people or $150) each way. *See page 111 for restaurants on St. John.*

Note: Ferries leave Cruz Bay on the top of the hour from 6 a.m. until 11 p.m. If you miss this last one, well...you're on St. John for the night.

77

GOLF, TENNIS & FITNESS CENTERS

GOLF

George and Tom Fazio designed this championship 18-hole, 6022 yard, par 70 golf course at **Mahogany Run** *(800.253.7103 or 340.777.6006)* on the north side of the island.

The course is certainly one of the best-maintained courses in the Caribbean and the "Devils Triangle"—the 13th, 14th, and 15th holes—challenges the golfer to drive right over the Caribbean sea from atop a cliff.

TENNIS

There are some free public courts on the island, but whether you are looking for a lesson or just some court time, you are better off calling **Marriott Frenchman's Reef** *(340.776.8500)* and **Wyndham Sugar Bay** *(340.777.7100)* which all have courts available for a nominal fee to nonguests.

FITNESS CENTERS

When you feel the need for a workout, the following places have weight machines, free weights, treadmills, stair climbers, bicycles, and even personal trainers.

Carib Health Complex at Sub Base *(340.777.1072)*

Gold's Gym (yes, just like in the States) next to the Harley Davidson in Charlotte Amalie *(340.777.9474)*.

CHAPTER 6

GREAT ST. THOMAS BEACHES & WATERSPORTS

"Babies don't need a vacation, but
I still see them at the beach."
—*Steven Wright*

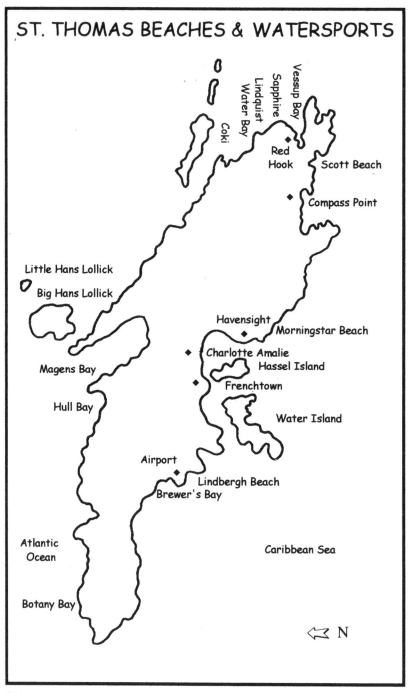

ST. THOMAS BEACHES & WATERSPORTS

Vessup Bay
Sapphire
Lindquist
Water Bay
Coki
Red Hook
Scott Beach
Compass Point
Little Hans Lollick
Big Hans Lollick
Havensight
Morningstar Beach
Charlotte Amalie
Hassel Island
Magens Bay
Frenchtown
Hull Bay
Water Island
Airport
Lindbergh Beach
Brewer's Bay
Atlantic Ocean
Caribbean Sea
Botany Bay
N

GREAT BEACHES

St. Thomas has many great beaches. Some are undeveloped. Others are in front of resorts. On St. Thomas, as in all the USVI, all beaches are open to everyone, even if there's a resort fronting the beach. Bear in mind that a resort beach is groomed at least once day. Workers pick up trash and rake the sand. Anyone used to a groomed beach can think a natural beach in the Caribbean looks "messy," but it's not really. It's just that there's no one around to remove the seaweed or pick up the detritus tossed onshore by the waves. Remember that weekends are by far the busiest beach days in these islands.

BOTANY BAY BEACH
It's way out at the western tip of the island, a very long drive and then a bit of a walk, but the snorkeling is quite good here.

BREWER'S BAY BEACH
This beach is west of the airport (keep the airport on the left as you drive west on Brewer's Bay Drive—Rte. 30, and then drive all the way through the University of the Virgin Islands campus). This is a calm swimming beach and there are several snack trucks here on weekends. It's close to the final approach to the airport and a great place to see planes of all sizes.

COKI BEACH
At the eastern end of the island, right next to Coral World, lies this popular beach. It's usually calm and there is good snorkeling around the cluster of rocks at the eastern end of the beach.

HULL BAY BEACH
You'll see lots of little painted fishing boats bouncing at their buoys at this small north shore beach. It's not a great swimming beach because there are so many little boats and it can be rough when the surf is up. There's a popular barefoot bar a bit behind the beach with weekend entertainment. The menu ranges from hot dogs to sandwiches to linguini with meat sauce.

LINDBERGH BEACH
Practically across the street from the airport, this nice long beach is great for walking and is also a calm swimming beach. Not very many large planes fly in and out of St. Thomas so the airport noise really isn't a problem. There are several hotels here and you can rent jet skis and waverunners and go waterskiing here. There's also some fine food to be had at the little snack bar wagons parked along the road.

LINDQUIST BEACH

Also called Smith Bay Beach, it's on the eastern shore and one of the few easily accessible beaches that is undeveloped (although plans loom). This is a long beach great for swimming and walking. From Smith Bay Road (between Pavilions and Pools and Wyndham Sugar Bay) two dirt roads lead to the beach. One is a minute north of Pavilions and Pools, quite bumpy, and can involve encounters with cows. The less bumpy, easier (no cows) dirt road is just a few yards farther. From Red Hook, look for the green airport sign. Heading to Red Hook, look for the yellow barrier.

MAGENS BAY BEACH

Year after year this stunning north shore beach is voted one of the world's ten most beautiful beaches, and it's both popular and easy to reach. It was donated to St. Thomas by Arthur S. Fairchild in 1946 to be preserved forever as a public park. The beach is a very long gentle curve of dazzling white sand and the water is exceptionally calm. There's a cafeteria-style snack bar and a large beach shop and you can rent chairs, floats, towels, snorkel gear, and lockers. *$1 per vehicle and $3 per person entrance fee.*

MORNINGSTAR BEACH

Just outside of St. Thomas harbor, this beach is at Marriott Frenchman's Reef and Morning Star Resorts and there are several restaurants and bars here. You can rent beach chairs, snorkel and windsurfing equipment, and take windsurfing and sunfish lessons. The beach is fairly long and generally calm, but it can have a swell with certain winds.

SAPPHIRE BEACH AND PELICAN BEACH

This half-mile-long beach fronts the Sapphire Beach Resort on the east end of St. Thomas. You can parasail, rent waverunners and sunfish, take windsurfing and scuba lessons, and rent floats and chairs. **Pelican Beach** is adjacent to the north and much quieter. Just scramble over the rocks.

SCOTT BEACH

You'll find this beach at the southeastern end of the island near Compass Point. You can rent beach lounges and umbrellas.

VESSUP BAY BEACH

This quiet, eastern beach near Cabrita Point is usually calm for swimming.

WATER BAY BEACH

This 1,000-foot-long, eastern beach is very calm and good for swimming.

GREAT WATERSPORTS

St. Thomas offers practically every watersport imaginable. You can snorkel, take out a sunfish, go for a sail, scuba dive day or night, try your hand at parasailing, hop onto a jet ski or a waverunner, paddle a kayak, or pedal a pedal boat. You can also rent a little powerboat or charter a boat and visit beaches on other islands, and you can even boat to the BVI for a day (see page 94). *St. Thomas is a particularly great place to try a watersport for the very first time. Watersports centers here, more so than on most islands, really do specialize in teaching the beginner as well as outfitting the expert.*

JET SKIS AND WAVERUNNERS

You can skim over the waves at many locations around the island of St. Thomas. Two popular spots to rent jet skis are **Marriott Frenchman's Reef Resort** *(340.776.8500)* and **Sapphire Beach Resort Marina** *(340.690.1775)*.

KAYAKING

In the Virgin Islands, there are actually two kinds of kayaking. Many resorts have brightly colored one- and two-person "kayaks" which are fun to take out and paddle about. The kayaking sport is also popular in the Virgin Islands. You can rent real kayaks and join kayaking trips. The waters off the east end of St. Thomas have many uninhabited islands and coves you can explore. Call **West Indies Wind Surfing** at Vessup Bay Beach *(340.775.6530; call first to make an appointment)*. They rent kayaks and have kites that catch the wind and propel you; but don't let the wind take you too far in one direction or you'll have a long paddle back.

KAYAKING PLUS SNORKELING

Kayak into Mangrove Lagoon with naturalists from **Virgin Island Ecotours** *(340.779.2155)* and then snorkel and see juvenile reef fish, upside-down jellyfish, barracuda, and rays. Or kayak to Cas Cay for a great snorkel and a gentle hike to a blow hole and a marine tidal pool. If you've never snorkeled, you'll find great teachers here. The Cas Cay trip is also available via a boat if you prefer not to kayak.

PARASAILING

Want to take a ride 400 feet above the water? This popular sport is easy to do. You don't even have to get wet. You're strapped into a parachute, a speedboat surges forward, and up you go! Boats will pick you up at many locations. Call **Caribbean Parasailing** *(340.775.9360)*.

PEDAL BOATS

Quite a few resorts have these little contraptions. They look a bit silly but once you're in one, they can be fun. Basically two people sit in a floating set of chairs and pedal around. It's interesting to look back at the shore and a slow trip takes almost no energy. Do bring a soda or a pina colada.

POWERBOATS

On calm days it can be wonderful fun to rent your own little powerboat and tool around in the water, or find a good snorkeling spot, or explore the uninhabited islands off the east end of St. Thomas. You can take a picnic to Lavango or Mingo Cay or even head over to a beach on St. John. If it's really calm and you feel like an adventure, you can also head to the BVI (you'll need a passport). **Nauti Nymph** *(340.775.5066)* in Red Hook offers 25', 29', and 31' center console boats and catamarans with bimini tops, built-in ice coolers, swim ladders, VFH radios, charts, and safety gear. **Pocket Yachts** (340.690.6015) at Sapphire Marina rents 22' to 30' boats with similar features. Both companies rent snorkel gear, too.

SCUBA DIVING

St. Thomas is surrounded by lots of good diving sites. If you've always wanted to try diving, now is a good time. It's possible to take a resort course and actually dive the same day. Call **Chris Sawyer Diving Center** *(340.777.7804)* at Red Hook or the **St. Thomas Diving Club** *(340.776.2381)* at Bolongo Bay Resort.

SNORKELING

Snorkeling equipment (mask, fins, snorkel) is available at virtually all resorts on St. Thomas and can be rented on many beaches. The water is clear here and you will see many colorful little fish. First-timers may want to try snorkeling right off the beach where it's sandy—you'll probably see some fish and you can practice breathing—slow and steady is the key. Once you can breathe easily, swim over to the rocky areas and see what is going on. If you want to go on a snorkeling trip (there are many to choose from) call the **Charterboat Center** *(340.775.7990)* and they'll match you with a trip that is right for you.

WINDSURFING

Lots of people spend hours trying to stay on these things. If you don't feel like trying it yourself, find a good spot on the beach where you can watch someone else try. It's often very funny. Most resorts rent windsurfing equipment and also give lessons or call **Carib Board Sailing** *(340.776.1730)* or **West Indies Windsurfing** *(340.755.6530)*.

GREAT DAY TRIPS ON, UNDER, AND OVER THE WATER

AN ELEGANT BOAT TRIP

Let's start on the water aboard **Magic Moments**, a 45' Sea Ray Express Cruiser. The morning begins with an onboard French continental breakfast followed by snorkeling at a few special and specially selected snorkeling spots (depending on the wind and the weather). Then an elegant lunch of lobster etoufe, assorted meats and cheeses, fine wines and freshly baked French bread. Then some time to float or explore or just chill and catch the views and the breezes before a final stop at Jost Van Dyke's Soggy Dollar Bar. Then it's back to your base. All in all a very good day in Paradise. *340.775.5066, 800.734.7345.*

SEEING EYE TO EYE WITH SOME GLORIOUS FISH

Now, under the water on **Submarine Atlantis**. This journey begins with a twenty-minute boat ride out to the air-conditioned 65' submarine. Once you board, it descends 80 feet under the sea, and the scenes through your viewports are spectacular. Sea turtles, parrot fish, sergeant majors, queen angelfish, and yellow-tail snapper are just a few of the many creatures you might see. You will be under water for about fifty minutes and the complete excursion lasts about two hours. *340.776.5650,866.546.7820.*

A STUNNING VIEW FROM ABOVE

And finally over the sea and land on a **Blue Water Aviation** helicopter. Helicopter flights to the British Virgin Islands, St. Croix, St. Martin and other islands leave from Cyril King airport. Blue Waters also offers sight-seeing flights of the U.S. and British Virgins and special occasion packages for weddings, birthdays, anniversaries, or anything else. It's your ticket to a true birds-eye-view of the islands. *340.776.5631.*

SOME HELPFUL HINTS

DRIVING AROUND THE ISLAND

St. Thomas is an island of spectacularly steep hills and the views up top are simply stunning. It's definitely worth it to take a drive around the island. It's nice to have the freedom of a car, but consider taking a taxi tour first—to get your bearings, to get a sense of local driving habits and the steepness of the roads, and to be able to concentrate on the scenery instead of the curves.

WHAT, NO ELECTRICITY?

Don't worry when the electricity suddenly goes off. It happens all the time and it's no big deal. (That's why you have a candle in your hotel room.) You don't even have to be very patient as the power almost always comes right back on in just a few minutes. Don't worry. Be happy.

INVISIBLE BUGS WITH A BITE

Around sundown, especially when it is not windy, very annoying little 'no-see-ums' appear out of nowhere and bite. Insect repellent generally keeps them at bay and wind keeps them away. For some people, these bites have a lasting itch and it's good to have a medication like Sting-Eze around. A dab of gin will work in a pinch.

FERRY BOATS TO OTHER ISLANDS

Ferries to St. John and the British Virgin Islands leave from Red Hook and several spots along the waterfront at Charlotte Amalie. Ferries to St. Croix leave only from the Charlotte Amalie waterfront (see page 141 for schedules).

CHAPTER 7

GREAT
ST. THOMAS
ATTRACTIONS

"There are more than ninety-nine steps
to these ninety-nine steps."

—Peter P., age 9
from Visiting the Virgin Islands with the Kids

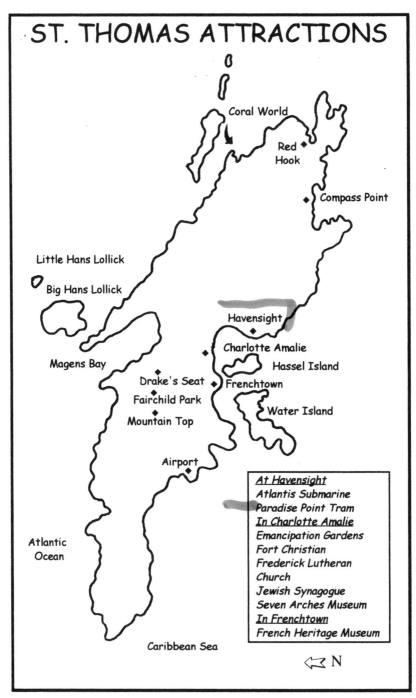

ST. THOMAS ATTRACTIONS

Coral World

Red
Hook

Compass Point

Little Hans Lollick

Big Hans Lollick

Havensight

Charlotte Amalie

Hassel Island

Magens Bay

Drake's Seat

Frenchtown

Fairchild Park

Water Island

Mountain Top

Airport

Atlantic
Ocean

At Havensight
Atlantis Submarine
Paradise Point Tram
In Charlotte Amalie
Emancipation Gardens
Fort Christian
Frederick Lutheran
Church
Jewish Synagogue
Seven Arches Museum
In Frenchtown
French Heritage Museum

Caribbean Sea

N

HISTORICAL SIGHTS

There is much more to Charlotte Amalie than shopping. The town is listed in the National Register of Historic Places for its history and for its architecture. Below are descriptions of some of the most interesting buildings. If you want more information, you can find a nice selection of books and pamphlets and an excellent walking tour for sale in the Virgin Islands Museum shop at Fort Christian.

EMANCIPATION GARDEN

This is the park right in front of the Grand Galleria and is dedicated to the emancipation of the slaves in the Danish West Indies on July 3, 1848. Many local celebrations and events are held here. *Grand Galleria.*

FRENCH HERITAGE MUSEUM

This delightful museum is housed in a colorful yellow cottage in Frenchtown. Its displays, documents, photographs, and artifacts chronicle the history and lives of St. Thomians of French descent throughout the island's history. It is a simple museum with many interesting items and definitely worth a visit. *Donations welcome. 340714.2583, 340.774.2320. Mon.-Sat. 9 a.m.-6 p.m. Frenchtown, two blocks west of the Post Office.*

FORT CHRISTIAN

You'll spot this red brick National Historic Landmark the first time you come to town. They've been restoring it for what seems like forever and there's still more to do. It's the earliest known building in town and construction probably started around 1666. When the exhibits are open, you can learn about famous local people, see examples of furniture that was typically in homes here 100 years ago, check out exhibits of shells, local fauna and flora, and birds. During the school year there are ever-changing exhibits by local students. The museum hours are sporadic during renovations. Be sure to call. *Donations welcome. 340.776.4566. Waterfront Hwy. Entrance around back.*

FREDERICK EVANGELICAL LUTHERAN CHURCH

This lovely church was established here in 1666 and the present building was started in 1789. A wide yellow brick stairway leads up to the arched entranceway. The ceiling of the church is dramatically arched and the wood in the chancel and pulpit is local mahogany. *Free. On Main Street, two blocks east of the Post Office.*

89

JEWISH SYNAGOGUE

Founded in 1796, this is the oldest Hebrew house of worship in continuous use under the U.S. flag. The benches and ark are fashioned out of local mahogany. The floor is sand, symbolic of a time when Jews in Spain were forced to practice their religion in secrecy and did so in cellars, using sand to muffle the sound. The walls here are made of bricks held together by sand, limestone, and molasses and it is said that years earlier children used to lick the walls to get a taste of the sweet molasses. *Donations accepted. Crystal Gade at Raadets Gade.*

SEVEN ARCHES MUSEUM

Ring the bell at the imposing black iron gate and you'll be invited in to this restored private house, built with yellow ballast bricks from Denmark. Look at the stone oven in the original Danish kitchen. This is what people used to cook everything in, from stews and roasts to loaves of bread. Kids of all ages will like climbing up the steps to the high porch and seeing the many iguanas roaming about. *Small donation requested. 340.774.9295. Follow Main St. east past Government House to the sign on the left. Follow the sign halfway down the alley.*

ATTRACTIONS AROUND THE ISLAND

St. Thomas has a number of tourist attractions and some of them really are quite special. Mountain Top and Drake's Seat are popular stops for the cruise ship crowds, but you can see them without the throngs if you go in the early morning or late afternoon. Very early morning is a great time to catch the views and take stunning photographs at scenic places that are always open, like Drake's Seat.

CORAL WORLD

The advertising can make this cluster of white geodesic domes look too "touristy" but what you see here is great and definitely worth a trip. So, what do you see? The **Underwater Observatory** lets you look right into a real reef. Circular stairs lead down into an underwater room ringed with windows that look right into the ocean. You see the surface up above and all kinds of fish and underwater plants and corals, all in their natural habitat. It's like snorkeling without getting wet! You'll spot live lobsters hiding in the rocks, shimmering silvery waves of giant schools of tiny fish moving as one, and fish hovering just outside the window, gawking at you.

The **Marine Gardens is** a collection of individual aquariums showcasing sea life up close. Check out the incredibly delicate little seahorses, corals that glow in the dark, burrowing jawfish, and moray eels. Kids of all ages get a kick out of patting a baby shark at the **Shark Shallows,** feeding stingrays at the **Stingray Pool,** and touching stuff in the "Touch Pond" which has all kinds of sea creatures including some weird ones—a sea cucumber that spits, a worm that goes inside itself. **Sea Trekkin'** is for anyone over eight (and over 80 pounds). Wear your bathing suit, don a special Coral World helmet, and roam the ocean floor in this guided undersea tour. Reservations are a must. If you hate crowds, go later in the day. You'll miss the talks and feedings but you'll be almost alone. *340.775.1555. $18 adult, $9 children 3-12, $52 family pass (2 adults, up to 4 children). Sea Trekkin' additional fee. Daily 9 a.m.–5 p.m. Coki Point.*

DRAKE'S SEAT

Legend has it that Sir Francis Drake used this place as a lookout to spot enemy Spanish fleets. It's now a parking area with a truly spectacular view of Magens Bay. Vendors selling T-shirts and such are here during cruise ship hours and and kids can have their photo taken with a delightful donkey decked out in bougainvillaea blossoms. Come here early morning or late afternoon to be alone and just absorb the stunning vista. *Rte. 40.*

FAIRCHILD PARK

A stone pathway and two benches offer spots for rest and relaxation from this very tiny, exquisitely peaceful park high up on a mountain. On a clear day, there's a spectacular, almost 360-degree view. *St. Peter Mountain Rd.*

MOUNTAIN TOP

Perched 1,547 feet above sea level, this rather touristy attraction is one of the highest, easily accessible points on St. Thomas and a good choice for a stunning view overlooking St. Thomas and Magens Bay and the British Virgin Islands. There's a little restaurant, a number of shops, and a bar that specializes in daiquiris. Bring your camera. *Off Rte. 33.*

PARADISE POINT TRAMWAY

Swiss-built gondolas carry you up 700 feet to the top of Flagg Hill and a spectacular view of Charlotte Amalie. The trip takes five minutes and stores plus a restaurant and bar await you; a perfect place to relax and admire the view. *340.774.9809. Daily 9 a.m.-5 p.m. Day Pass: $18 adults, children 6-12 $9. Across from Havensight.*

CHARTERING A YACHT

Think about it. Whether you're an old salt who might want to captain your own boat or a fair weather sailor who wants a captain and crew, the steady winds, calm Virgin Island waters, and line of sight navigation make this the ideal place for a nautical vacation.

With wonderful, sheltered anchorages and the availability of just about any vessel you might imagine—from traditional sailboats to catamarans to sport fishers and trawlers and even motor sailors—you can't go wrong.

An excellent place to find a great charter is **Admiralty Yacht Vacations.** *P.O. Box 306162, St. Thomas 00803. Res: 800.895.5808. Tel: 340.774.2172. Fax: 340.774.8010. www.admirals.com*

CATCHING THE BIG ONE

Chartering a yacht for a week is surely an adventure, but if you want to pack a whole bunch of on-the-sea excitement into one day, how about deep-sea fishing? Yes, a 1,282-pound blue marlin was caught in these waters a while back, but the average here is a mere 200-300 pounds.

The boats are in beautiful condition, the captains and crews are helpful, knowledgeable, and experienced and the excitement of the day can be an exhilarating and absolutely unforgettable event. Whether you're on St.. Thomas or St. John, you'll want Tyler Maltby or one of the other great fish finders of the **Double Header Sportfishing.** They've been one of the best in the Caribbean for 30 years.

Sapphire Beach Marina, St. Thomas. 340.777.7317. Fax: 430.775.6022. www.doubleheadersportfishing.net

St. Thomas Communications *(340.776.4324, 168 Crown Bay)* offers a full line of business services and computers and Internet access, but without the food and drink.

ST. JOHN
Connections on St. John *(Cruz Bay, a block from the ferry dock, 340.776.6922; Coral Bay by Skinny Legs, 340.779.4994)* offers many services including Federal Express and Western Union, phones, faxes, Internet access, and secretarial services.

Donkey Diner *(340.693.5240, in Coral Bay)* is a funky stop for an Internet connection.

Every Ting *(340.693.5820, south of Wharfside Village)* has a computer you can log onto (plus cappuccinos and more).

Quiet Mon *(340.779.4799, upstairs across from First Bank)* offers the chance to connect over a cold beer.

Surf da Web *(340.693.9152, 2nd floor at the Marketplace)* has an air-conditioned room full of computers waiting for you.

islands. You are taken directly to excellent snorkeling areas and an expert goes in the water with you. The exact routes and islands that you visit will depend on the weather and wind the day you go. **Captain Nautica** *(340.715.3379)* offers several terrific trips to the BVI. Boats leave from Red Hook and go to a variety of islands, depending on the weather. From St. Thomas or St. John, **Limnos Charters** *(340.775.3203)* has 53' twin engine, smooth-riding catamarans and takes up to 45 people, and **Stormy Petrel** and **Pirate's Penny** *(340.775.7990)* have 42' diesel single engine powerboats and take up to 12 people. These trips usually go along the north side of Tortola and on to the Virgin Gorda Baths and other islands for swimming and snorkeling.

THE BVI FROM THE WATER (PRIVATE CHARTER)
When you want to customize a snorkeling or beaching or even a hiking trip to the BVI, call **Dohm Water Taxi** *(340.775.6501)*. Their pilot/guides are incredibly knowledgeable and can take you places and show you things most people don't know about—like the underwater lava flows off Tortola. **Nauti Nymph** *(340.775.5066)* has captained private day charters to the BVI from St. Thomas and St. John. You can design your own itinerary or you can let the captain decide. The **Charterboat Center** *(340.775.7990; from the U.S. 800.866.5714)* is in Red Hook.

They specialize in trips to the British Virgin Islands and can arrange a variety of powerboat trips, sportfishing trips, day sails, and even weekly charters. If you're not sure what you want, they'll help you decide. Call ahead or stop by their offices.

RENTING YOUR OWN BOAT

This can be a great way to explore the beaches and snorkeling areas of the BVI. From St. Thomas you can reach Jost Van Dyke in 30 minutes, the Caves on Norman Island in 45 minutes, and The Baths on Virgin Gorda in 90 minutes. Everything is closer from St. John. However, unless you're an old salt, don't even think of doing this on a really windy day. You'll be wet, scared to death, bounced about, and it will take forever to get anywhere. You must have a passport and clear customs (town dock on Jost Van Dyke,Yacht Harbour on Virgin Gorda, West End or Road Town in Tortola). *See page 84 to rent a boat on St. Thomas, page 128 for St. John.*

PUBLIC FERRIES TO THE BVI

There are several ferry companies that connect St. Thomas and St. John to the BVI. **Road Town Fast Ferry** *(340.777.2800)* has a high speed catamaran that makes the Charlotte Amalie-Roadtown trip in 50 minutes. On regular ferries, it's a 30-minute trip from Red Hook, St. Thomas to West End, Tortola. Call **Transportation Services** *(340.776.6282)* or call **Varlack Ventures** *(340.776.6412)*. From Charlotte Amalie, it's a 45-minute trip to West End and 90 minutes to Road Town, Tortola. Call **Native Son** *(340.774.8685)* or **Smith's Ferry** *(340.775.7292; they also have a trip to Virgin Gorda every other Saturday)*. It's a 30-minute trip from Cruz Bay, St. John to West End, Tortola. Call **Inter-Island Ferry** *(340.776.6597)*. On Fridays, Saturdays, and Sundays, Inter-Island ferries take passengers to the island of Jost Van Dyke from Red Hook, St. Thomas and Cruz Bay, St. John. You'll have time to explore, swim, and visit little beach bars, including Foxy's. Once a month, and twice when there is a blue moon, Inter-Island ferries leave early in the evening for Bomba's famous all-night Full Moon Parties on Tortola. Go to www.stthomasthisweek.com for current ferry schedules.

A WEDDING IN PARADISE

Finding a more romantic, beautiful, and unforgettable setting for a wedding than either St. Thomas or St. John may not be possible. An added advantage is that you are already here for your honeymoon. It can be the wedding of the century with hundreds of guests, helicopters, sea planes, and submarines or a simple ceremony on a deserted beach or a tranquil mountain top.

The actual logistics, legalities, and application process is quite simple and you can explore it yourselves by calling 340.774.6680. But whatever your plans you can get ideas, help, and moral support from a professional wedding planner. Most of the larger hotels have their own in-house wedding planners and there are a number of wonderful independent planners.

You can tell them exactly what you want and they can make it happen, or you can call on their years of experience to give you some new ideas. Either way these professionals can handle everything from location to catering to favors, flowers, photographers, and formal wear. Some of the favorite resorts for weddings on St. Thomas are the St. Thomas Ritz-Carlton *(340.775.3333),* Marriot Frenchman's Reef/Morningstar Beach *(340.776.8500),* and Bolongo Bay Beach Resort *(340.449.1577).* On St. John you can reach the Westin's Director of Romance *(340.693.8000, ext. 1908)* or try one of Caneel Bay's wedding packages *(340.776.6111).*

If you are looking for a simpler island wedding experience or a renewal of vows on St. Thomas, contact Colleen Mader at **Simple Island Weddings** *(340.774.0729 or 340.643.3979).* Or you can visit her Web site at www.simpleweddings.com. On St. John, **The Barefoot Minister**, Ann Marie Porter, *(888.676.5701 or 340.693.5153)* can see to all your wedding needs. Or visit her Web site at www.stjohnweddings.com.

SECTION II

ST. JOHN

**PLACES TO STAY
RESTAURANTS
BARS
SHOPPING
BEACHES
WATERSPORTS
LANDSPORTS
HISTORICAL ATTRACTIONS**

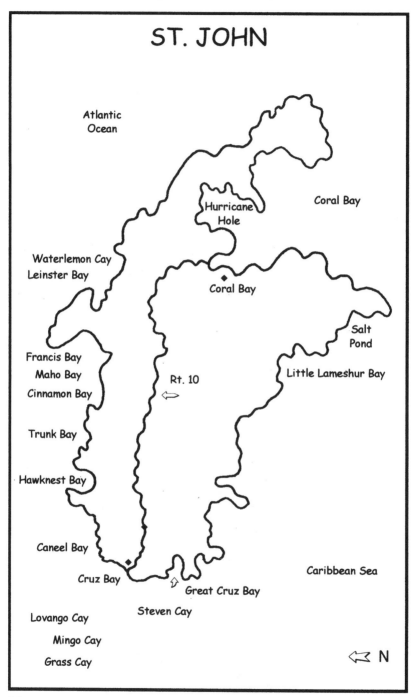

ST. JOHN

Atlantic
Ocean

Hurricane
Hole

Coral Bay

Waterlemon Cay
Leinster Bay

Coral Bay

Salt
Pond

Francis Bay
Maho Bay
Cinnamon Bay

Rt. 10

Little Lameshur Bay

Trunk Bay

Hawknest Bay

Caneel Bay

Cruz Bay

Great Cruz Bay

Caribbean Sea

Steven Cay

Lovango Cay

Mingo Cay

Grass Cay

N

ABOUT ST. JOHN

St. John is a true one-of-a-kind destination and, in a way, has a bit of everything. The island is only 20 square miles and has a population of only 4,200, yet it entices an unusually wide assortment of visitors.

Two-thirds of St. John is part of the U.S. National Park system and the island is extraordinarily untouched. This is an island with terrific hiking trails, numerous exquisite beaches, and superb snorkeling. It's a wonderful place to explore and it's a real outdoor paradise. There are even great campgrounds. However, St. John is also home to a very U.S. mainland-style, full-service resort and to a sophisticated luxury retreat, both of which you never have to leave. There are also a few other lodging choices and villas to rent all over the island.

St. John is much more isolated than St. Thomas. There's no airport here. You fly to St. Thomas and then take a ferry. Everything on St. John is on a much smaller scale than St. Thomas and it's a much, much quieter island. St. John is the place to come if you want to spend your days exploring the island by jeep, if you like to hike, if you want to lie on pristine beaches, or if you hope to find many wonderful snorkeling spots. It's a good island to come to if you wish to get away from crowds and do things on your own. And it's a place to come if you want to go to little bars, dine outside on gourmet cuisine, or just want to munch a grilled cheese sandwich. Restaurants and bars are mostly casual, open-air, and small, yet you can also find very sophisticated cuisine. You can be as casual or as formal as you want.

The western end of St. John, including the little town of Cruz Bay, is the busier side of the island. Cruz Bay is where the ferries dock and where you will find most of St. John's bars, restaurants, and shops. The eastern end of the island, and its tiny settlement of Coral Bay, is very isolated. St. John is extremely hilly but main roads are well maintained and the drives are just amazing. Roads run through forests and under canopies of trees, climb alarmingly and drop precipitously, and there are some dicey hairpin curves, but the views and vistas are spectacular, switching back and forth from completely pristine steep green hills to shimmering seas dotted with islands.

SOME GREAT PEOPLE, SOME GREAT BEER

Even if you're not really a beer drinker and especially if you are, there is nothing quite like an icy, icy cold beer in the islands. When the air temperature hovers around 85 degrees and the beer temperature hovers around 35 degrees, that is an "island beer experience." And if your choice of beers is Foxy's Lager or Blackbeard's Ale or Virgin Islands Pale Ale then you're really chillin' with de island beer, mon.

Foxy's Lager, named for Jost Van Dyke's legendary entrepreneur, entertainer, and party person, and Blackbeards, named for the infamous pirate, are products of the Virgin Islands Brewing Company and brewed by the Minnesota Brewing Company in St. Paul.

Virgin Island's Pale Ale was actually created and perfected on St. John by two expats Kevin Chipman and Chirag "Cheech" Vyas and is now brewed for the St. John Brewing Company by Shipyard Brewer Company in Portland Maine.

Kevin and Cheech were trying to create a less watery-tasting beer, a brew that might capture a bit of the magic of these islands. It appears they have succeeded. Virgin Island's Pale Ale is a crisp, lighter ale with a subtle fruit aura, perhaps a perfect fit for the islands.

As the inimitable Mr. Chipman laments after a hard day: "I live in paradise. I make, sell, and drink beer for a living. Hey, somebody's got to do it."

Well, it must be time for an icy island brew!

CHAPTER 8

GREAT ST. JOHN PLACES TO STAY

"I never met a place like this
in my life."

—Hugh Benjamin
from A Place Like This

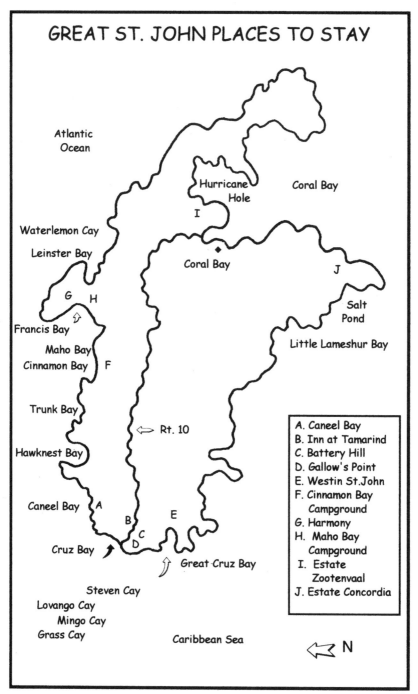

GREAT ST. JOHN PLACES TO STAY

Atlantic
Ocean

Hurricane
Hole

Coral Bay

I

Waterlemon Cay

Leinster Bay

Coral Bay

J

G   H

Salt
Pond

Francis Bay

Little Lameshur Bay

Maho Bay

Cinnamon Bay   F

Trunk Bay

⇦ Rt. 10

Hawknest Bay

A. Caneel Bay
B. Inn at Tamarind
C. Battery Hill
D. Gallow's Point
E. Westin St. John
F. Cinnamon Bay
    Campground
G. Harmony
H. Maho Bay
    Campground
I. Estate
    Zootenvaal
J. Estate Concordia

Caneel Bay   A

B   E
C
Cruz Bay   D

Great Cruz Bay

Steven Cay

Lovango Cay

Mingo Cay

Grass Cay   Caribbean Sea

⇦ N

GREAT ST. JOHN PLACES TO STAY

The Virgin Islands National Park covers more than two-thirds of St. John and much of the island is completely undeveloped. However, there are a number of wonderful lodging choices on the island and they run the gamut from full-service resorts all the way to campgrounds. You can stay near the little town of Cruz Bay or in the Virgin Islands National Park or in the remote east end. In addition, scattered about all over the island are delightful houses for rent by the week or by the month. **Rates are per night without meals for two people on-season (off-season in parentheses) and do not include the additional 8% room tax or hotel service charges or special fees.**

RENTING A HOUSE OR A VILLA

People talk about renting villas in the Caribbean, but actually what they mean most of the time is just a house. St. John has a wonderful variety of rental houses. You can get just about anything, from a very modest house with simple furnishings and no view and no pool (which is just fine if you plan to spend your days exploring beaches around the island) to an elegantly furnished many-bedroom villa with a large pool, stunning views, and maid and chef service. You will need to rent a car unless you plan to get groceries on the way in and never leave.

Rental houses are either on or above a beach, on the water and near a beach, or up in the hills. Although beachfront houses make it delightfully easy to go to the beach, remember that they are generally less private, simply because the beaches are public. Rental houses in the hills can have stunning views, and the higher up you go, the more breathtaking the scene, but bear in mind that St. John is incredibly hilly and roads are very steep. Before you rent, look at a map of St. John and decide what you'd like to be near, such as Cruz Bay or the north shore beaches or Coral Bay. Houses are rented by the week, and rates run all the way from $1,500 to $10,000.

Caribbean Villas & Resorts, *P.O. Box 458, Cruz Bay, 00831. Res: 800.338.0987. Tel: 340.776.6152. Fax: 340.779.4044. www.caribbeanvilla.com*
Destination St. John, *P.O. Box 8306, Cruz Bay, 00830. Res: 800.562.1901. Tel: 340.779.4647. Fax: 340.715.0073. www.destinationstjohn.com*
Suites St. John, *21604 Goshen Oaks Rd., Gaithersburg, MD 20882. Res: 800.348.8444. www.suitestjohn.com*

CANEEL BAY

If you want understated luxury and to combine hours of relaxing on very private beaches with elegant cuisine, you can't beat this longtime favorite.

Caneel Bay is on a 170-acre, vaguely hilly peninsula rimmed with seven stunning white sand beaches that are exceptionally private, because most of the property is accessible only to guests. The scenery here is spectacular. Peaceful paths lead to hammocks, benches, and quiet beaches across wide expanses of manicured green lawn radiant with blossoming hibiscus and bougainvillaea. From almost anywhere, you can see shades of azure Caribbean waters dotted with hilly, distant islands. Despite the fact that there are 166 units, beaches and paths can be remarkably empty.

Most rooms are in one- and two-story buildings that are beachfront but tucked discreetly behind sea grape trees. Others are waterfront or near the tennis courts. Rooms are inviting, expensively but casually decorated, and very comfortable. Some have stonework walls and spacious showers and all have air-conditioning, mini-bars, safes, coffee makers, irons, and robes. Children are welcome at Caneel Bay but two beaches (Scott and Paradise) are designated as "quiet beaches for those wishing to hear only the quiet lapping of the waves" and these beaches are off-limits to children who are under 13. The rooms behind these two beaches are one-story and designated as "premium" and have patios that look through the sea grapes to the beach. Meals are a pleasure at all of the restaurants and the cuisine is superb. Turtle Bay Estate House is especially elegant, even at breakfast.

Don't come here if you want a lot of action or if you want a TV or phone or data ports in your room or opulent Jacuzzi bathrooms. Caneel's luxury and elegance is subtle. You'll find it in the fine stonework arches, or the way the beachfront rooms have splendid water views yet are hidden in the sea grapes, so as not to spoil the untouched feel of the beach. This is one of the few luxury resorts left where you can actually leave the real world behind. Guests young and old come back year after year because for them, this kind of escape is one of the most relaxing and restorative experiences there is.

4 restaurants, bar, pool, 11 tennis courts, 7 beaches (excellent snorkeling), massage, fitness center, hiking, shop, cell phones on request, office center. Airport check-in and private ferry ($65 and includes unlimited trips to St. Thomas). Rates: $450-$875 ($350-$750). Special packages. 166 units. P.O. Box 720, Cruz Bay, 00831. Res: 800.928.8889. Tel: 340.776.6111. Fax: 340.693.8280. www.rosewood-hotels.com

GALLOWS POINT SUITE RESORT

Stay here for spectacular views and absolutely superb snorkeling all around the point. Cruz Bay is just a short walk away.

The land that wraps around the southern end of Cruz Bay ends with a rocky promontory known as Gallows Point. Fourteen gray, two-story, quadruplex condominiums are clustered here. From the water they appear almost too close to each other, but from the inside, tall, louvered doors completely fold back and showcase sensational views of turquoise waters and nearby islands and you completely forget that anyone could be right next door. All units have a separate bedroom, fully equipped kitchen, a living/dining area with a sleeper sofa, ceiling fans, air-conditioning, TV/VCR, and patio or balcony. Second-floor units are more spacious and have high ceilings over the living areas, loft bedrooms with a half-bath, and more dramatic views. All units have tile floors and are furnished in rattan and tropical prints. The pool and beach are quite tiny but the snorkeling is really superb all along the rocky shore heading away from Cruz Bay. ZoZo's *(see page 115),* the on-site restaurant, is excellent.
Restaurant, bar, small pool, tiny beach, shop, activities center. 60 units. Rates: $475-$575 ($275-$375). P.O. Box 58, Cruz Bay, 00831. Tel: 340.776.6434. Fax: 340.776.6520. Units managed by two companies. Res: 800.348.8444. www.gallowspoint.com and 800.323.7229. www.gallowspointresort.com

BATTERY HILL LUXURY SUITES

This small, hilltop condominium complex offers comfortable apartment living with a pool and you can walk to town.

Six apartments are in three buildings that peek out from the top of tropical foliage on a hilltop overlooking Cruz Bay. There is also a cottage. All units have a separate bedroom, a living-dining area, a fully equipped kitchen, TV/VCR, ceiling fans, and air-conditioning in the bedrooms. Each condominium is privately owned and decor varies, but generally you can count on tile floors, rattan furniture, and pastel print draperies, bedspreads, and cushions. Balconies catch the tropical breezes and are perfect spots to read or just gaze at the view and watch the harbor traffic in the distance. There's a nice size pool and Cruz Bay restaurants and shops are just a short walk down the hill.
Pool. 7 units. Rates: $240-$450 ($150-$295). P.O. 567, Cruz Bay, 00831. Res: 800.348.8444. www.suitestjohn.com/batteryhill

HARMONY STUDIOS

Kids and grown-ups alike get a kick out of this place, which is built entirely out of recycled materials.

Nestled among the trees above Maho Bay are these delightfully contemporary, comfortable duplex units built entirely out of recycled materials. You'd never guess what everything once was, even if you look very closely! Just for starters, the roof is made out of recycled cardboard, the doormat was fashioned out of melted old tires, the shiny walls were once newspapers, the shower tiles are created out of crushed light bulbs, and the outdoor furniture was originally soda bottles! Even some of the decor was once something else, like the throw rugs woven from plastic milk bottles. Don't be alarmed. Nothing even vaguely resembles what it once was and these units are very comfortable and attractive. Studios come in two sizes. In either size, the upstairs units have better views, more of a breeze, and cathedral ceilings. All units have kitchenettes (low voltage refrigerator, of course), spacious decks, and spectacular views. There's a beautiful beach down the hill. This is one of ecologist Stanley Selengut's marvelous brainstorms.

12 units. Rates: $205-$230 ($120-$145). P.O. Box 310, Cruz Bay, 00831. Res: 800.392.9004. Tel: 340.776.6240. Fax: 340.776.6504. www.maho.org

THE INN AT TAMARIND COURT

This very simple 20-room "bed and breakfast" has its own popular restaurant and is conveniently just a few steps up the hill from Cruz Bay.

As you enter the courtyard and see the little fountain, the bar, and the umbrella-shaded tables and chairs, you begin to sense you are in the midst of Caribbean casual. This recently refurbished "in town" basic inn has 20 smallish rooms, all with air-conditioning, cable television, small refrigerators, and daily maid service. The inn offers two suites for up to four guests, standard rooms for one or two, and economy singles that share a bath. (Very European.) The on-site restaurant (closed Sat.) offers breakfast and a different theme for dinner each night, from Italian to sushi to barbecue. The bar is a favorite gathering place for locals and tourists alike. A caring management, sensible prices, and convenient location make this a popular choice for those happy with quite basic accommodations.

Bar, restaurant. 20 units. Rates: $75-$240 ($60-$170). P.O. Box 350, Cruz Bay, 00831. Res: 800.221.1637. Tel: 340.776.6378. Fax: 340.776.6722. www.tamarindcourt.com

WESTIN ST. JOHN RESORT & VILLAS

Busy and bustling, this full-service resort is the most stateside-like lodging on St. John and both honeymooners and families flock here.

This resort is set on 47 acres that sweep down to a long crescent of white sand and look out to a harbor of sailboats gently rocking at anchor. Colorful two-story buildings cascade down to the beach, separated by green lawns, rows of palm trees, well-tended beds of brilliant tropical flowers, and broad brick walkways. Rooms are contemporary and spacious. Walls are painted in soft colors and prints hang on the walls. All rooms have signature Westin "Heavenly" beds and showers plus mini-bars, TV and in-room movies, safes, coffee makers, robes, and irons. The closer you are to the beach, the better the water view.

Up on the hill and open to the breezes is Chloe & Bernard's, the resort's fine dining restaurant *(see page 114)*. Down facing the beach is the Beach Cafe & Bar, open for breakfast, lunch, and dinner plus a lavish Sunday brunch. There's a very casual lunch and snack stop near the pool plus a poolside bar. A complete deli provides sandwiches, cookies, sodas, and assorted chips and dips. Room service is offered round-the-clock, including pizza to munch on while you watch an exciting in-room movie.

Activities center around the 1,200-foot beach and the quarter-acre, geometric-shaped pool, complete with two Jacuzzis and a small waterfall. The watersports center offers windsurfing, snorkeling, jet skiing, parasailing, plus fishing, sailing, and scuba trips. A car rental company is on the property.

The beach and the pool keep children busy but there is also an outstanding Teen Center and a great Kids Club which offers children ages three to 12 a full range of indoor and outdoor activities for a fee. It's open for half-day, full-day, and evening sessions and kids learn island arts and crafts, find out all about iguanas, and get involved in beach activities and volleyball games. Nestled among trees and dense foliage are 67 vacation villas available for rent or vacation ownership. Some have private pools.

3 restaurants, 3 bars, pool, beach, 6 tennis courts, fitness center, spa, 2 shops, deli. Airport check-in and private ferry ($65 per person, $45 ages 4-12; includes unlimited trips to St. Thomas). 285 units. Rates: $469-$669 ($259-$339) plus $25 per night resort charge. Special packages. P.O. Box 8310, Cruz Bay, 00831. Res: 888.627.7206. Tel: 340.693.8000. Fax: 340.779.4985. www.westinresortstjohn.com

EAST END LODGING

The settlement at the east end of St. John is the very tiny town of Coral Bay. It is about a 20-minute very hilly drive from Cruz Bay and quite isolated. Spread along the shore are a few delightful and very ultracasual restaurants, a deli, a market, and some shops.

ESTATE CONCORDIA STUDIOS & ECO-TENTS

These two adjacent properties are award-winning examples of ecologically sensitive developments.

Ten bumpy minutes past Coral Bay (and a good 45 minutes from Cruz Bay) you'll come to one of environmentalist Stanley Selengut's appealing creations. Nine studios and two-story duplexes and 11 eco-tents are tucked into the hillside in this very remote part of St. John. Units have a variety of configurations but all have full or partial ocean views and efficiency or full kitchens. The eco-tents have comforts that bring staying here a big notch above regular camping.

Pool. 9 studios and duplexes, 18 eco-tents. Rates for studios: $140-$215 ($95-$150). Rates for eco-tents: $155-$175 ($95). P.O. Box 310, Cruz Bay, 00831. Res: 800.392.9004. Tel: 340.776.6226. Fax: 340.776.6504. www.maho.org

ESTATE ZOOTENVAAL

These simple cottages are the ideal place to come when you want a peaceful, remote, "no frills" type of getaway and great snorkeling.

Three whitewashed bungalows are set along a low hill across the road from the water, each with a patio and spacious yard. Interiors are basic but very clean and extremely well kept. Well-placed louvres bring in the sea breezes and keep the cottages cool (and you can sleep to the sound of the lapping waves). Cook a gourmet meal in the full kitchen or stick to the simple life here. It's your choice. Across the street stairs lead down to a little, somewhat rocky beach on Hurricane Hole Bay. Estate Zootenvaal and the bay are within the Virgin Islands National Park boundaries and no boats are allowed to anchor in the bay which means the waters are undisturbed and the snorkeling is superb. Coral Bay establishments are just a few minutes away.

3 units. Maid service extra. Weekly rates for two people: one bedroom $1,925 (extra person $560), two bedroom $2,310 (each extra person $630). Daily rates available. General Manager: Robin Clair. Hurricane Hole, 00830. Tel: 340.776.6321. www.estatezootenvaal.com

CAMPGROUNDS
CINNAMON BAY CAMPGROUND

Here, rustic cottages, tents, and bare sites are hidden in the trees just minutes from a gorgeous white sand beach.

Cinnamon Bay, part of the Virgin Islands National Park, is St. John's longest beach. Set back against the hills and concealed among the tropical foliage, is this superb campground. The three types of accommodations are all within a two-minute walk from the beach and come with picnic tables and charcoal grills. Choose from screen-lined, 15' by 15' "cottages," with electric lights, ceiling fan, four twin beds and linens (changed twice weekly), propane gas stove, ice chest, cooking and eating utensils; canvas 10' by 14' tents on a solid floor, with a gas lantern, cots, linens (changed twice weekly), propane gas stove, ice chest, cooking and eating utensils; and bare sites, which can handle one large tent or two smaller tents. Bathrooms are nearby and there are public phones, a message center, safe deposit boxes, and lockers. Breakfast and lunch are served at a snack bar and the open-air restaurant Tree Lizards dishes up seafood, barbecues, and vegetarian delights every evening and even West Indian music on-season. The Beach Shop and Activities Deck arranges snorkeling, windsurfing, sea kayaking, and sailboat rentals, plus sailing cruises and scuba and snorkeling trips. Winter months fill up as far as a year in advance.
Restaurant, snack bar, beach, grocery store, gift shop. 126 units. Rates: cottages $110-$140 ($70-$90), tents $80 ($58), bare sites $27. P.O. Box 720, Cruz Bay, 00831. Res: 800.539.9998. Tel: 340.776.6330. Fax: 340.776.6458. www.cinnamonbay.com

MAHO BAY CAMPGROUND

Come here for hillside camping on a small but beautiful beach.

Fourteen acres of seemingly pristine forested hillside rise up from a classic, white sand beach, but hidden among the trees are clusters of open-sided, 16' by 16' tent cottages. It's amazing how very undisturbed the land is. Stairs and elevated walkways wind around trunks, interrupting nothing. This was Stanley Selengut's first ecological venture on St. John. Beds, tables, chairs, propane stoves, and cooking utensils are provided. Some tents have superb water views. There's an outdoor restaurant for breakfast and dinner, nightly entertainment on-season, a store, an art gallery, and an activities desk for sailing, snorkeling, windsurfing, and other watersports.
Restaurant. 114 units. Rates: $130 ($75). P.O. Box 310, Cruz Bay, 00831. Res: 800.392.9004. Tel: 340.693.6596. Fax: 340.776.6504. www.maho.org

HISTORICAL ATTRACTIONS ON ST. JOHN

ANNABERG SUGAR MILL

This sugar mill operated well into the late 1800s and these ruins are well preserved and a delight to visit. The National Park brochure identifies the buildings, describes how sugar was produced, and even names fruit trees. The view of the British Virgin Islands from here is superb. Periodically there are historical reenactments and island baking and cooking demonstrations. *340.776.6201. Rte. 20, near Leinster Bay.*

ELAINE IONE SPRAUVE LIBRARY AND MUSEUM

Built in 1757, this former Great House is now a library and a museum, with a small collection of Indian pottery and artifacts from ancient and colonial days. There are permanent exhibits on Danish West Indian history, natural history, and arts and crafts. Come here also to see ever-changing exhibits of work by local artists. *Open weekdays 9-5. 340.776.6359. Cruz Bay.*

IVAN JADAN MUSEUM

Ivan Jadan, considered one of the greatest Russian tenors of all time, spent his last 40 years on St. John. He died in 1995 and his wife has lovingly created this museum, a tribute to the classical singer's 92-year life and love for music. Historic photos, documents, and items are on display and there are numerous books you are welcome to read and you can listen to some of his performances, too, including the posthumously released CD, "Songs of the Heart." *Mon.-Sat. 9-11, 4-6, and by appointment. 340.776.6423. Genip St., Cruz Bay.*

CHAPTER 9

GREAT
ST. JOHN
RESTAURANTS
&
BARS

"Only Irish coffee provides in a single glass
all four essential food groups:
alcohol, caffeine, sugar, and fat."

—*Anonymous*

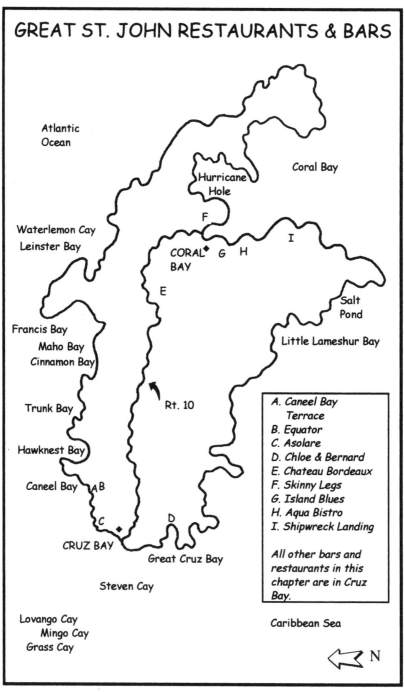

GREAT ST. JOHN RESTAURANTS & BARS

Atlantic
Ocean

Coral Bay

Hurricane
Hole

F

Waterlemon Cay
Leinster Bay

CORAL ◆ G H
BAY

I

E

Salt
Pond

Francis Bay
Maho Bay
Cinnamon Bay

Little Lameshur Bay

Trunk Bay

Rt. 10

Hawknest Bay

Caneel Bay   A B

C

D

CRUZ BAY

Great Cruz Bay

Steven Cay

A. Caneel Bay
   Terrace
B. Equator
C. Asolare
D. Chloe & Bernard
E. Chateau Bordeaux
F. Skinny Legs
G. Island Blues
H. Aqua Bistro
I. Shipwreck Landing

All other bars and
restaurants in this
chapter are in Cruz
Bay.

Lovango Cay
   Mingo Cay
Grass Cay

Caribbean Sea

N

GREAT ST. JOHN RESTAURANTS & BARS

One of the most magical and enchanting features of the Caribbean is the ability to have elegant meals on terraces that are open to the outdoors, to combine a sophisticated and refined style of dining with soft breezes and romantic nighttime scenery—sparkling stars, rising moons, twinkling distant lights.

While St. Thomas restaurants often are indoors and professionally decorated, even the finest St. John restaurants rely on the outdoor scenery and island breezes to create an inviting background for an elegant meal. In fact, it is possible to walk by a great restaurant on St. John in the afternoon and see only a stack of chairs on a concrete slab, and a padlock on the kitchen door. You just know that place must be closed for good. Yet return in the evening, and you'll find tablecloths, candlelight, and glistening wine buckets.

This chapter begins with St. John's elegant restaurants. Next are Cruz Bay casual restaurants and bars (which are all within walking distance of each other). Coral Bay restaurants and bars end the chapter. Bear in mind that off-season, hours and days of operation may vary and it is wise to call ahead. On-season, it's almost always necessary to make a dinner reservation at the fancier restaurants.

ST. JOHN'S FINEST RESTAURANTS

ASOLARE

The modest lattice and stonework entrance belies the stunning scenery that awaits you. This small, elegant, and wonderfully romantic restaurant is set high up on a hillside in a restored stone house and tables along the entire terrace look out to a spectacular panorama of azure waters and distant islands. After dark, the twinkling lights of Cruz Bay and St. Thomas are magical. The view alone would be worth the visit, but you'll find that the exquisitely presented, contemporary Asian cuisine is equally outstanding. Excellent dinner choices include the green tea citrus tuna, the grilled Peking duck breast, the seared beef filet Thai style, and the locally caught fresh fish of the day. Tables inside have much less of a view but are still quite romantic and the dark bar is a delight. *340.779.4747. A two-minute cab ride from Cruz Bay on Caneel Hill. D $$-$$$*

113

CANEEL BAY TERRACE

For elegant buffets with an outstanding array of selections—for lunch, dinner, and even breakfast—you can't beat the Caneel Bay Terrace at Caneel Bay resort. These buffets are among the very best anywhere and quite reasonably priced (for example, $25 for the lunch buffet, $22 for cold selections only). The cuisine is of the finest quality and the al fresco setting facing the bay is peaceful, with well-spaced tables. Numerous hot and cold items plus cooked-to-order choices are all beautifully presented. *Buffets breakfast and lunch Mon.-Sat., brunch Sun., dinner Mon. (Grand Buffet) and Wed. or Fri. Reservations for dinner essential (inquire about dress code). 340.776.6111. On Rte. 20, five minutes north of Cruz Bay. BLD $$*

CHATEAU BORDEAUX

This is about the highest place you can drive to on St. John and the attentive service and gourmet cuisine are a perfect match for the breathtaking, airplane-like views. Try to get here before dark so you can see the stunning colors at sunset time and the truly amazing vista of the British Virgin Islands. Starters include a caramelized onion, swiss chard, and goat cheese tart; a duck and chanterelle ravioli; and a grilled calamari salad. For entrees try the roasted pork loin with endive and sweet potato gnocchi, Caribbean bouillabaisse, or porcini-dusted mahi. Driving here in the dark is not for the faint of heart, so consider taking a cab unless you really know the road. Lunch is served on the outside deck and the simple menu includes burgers and daiquiris. *Reservations for dinner essential. 340.776.6611. Centerline Rd. at Carolina Hill. LD $$-$$$*

CHLOE & BERNARD'S

The decor is exotic at this independently run and very romantic restaurant at the Westin St. John. Gauzy fabric panels cascade from the cathedral ceiling and tables are nestled in dimly lit al fresco alcoves between giant pillars. The cuisine is multinational, including French, Swiss, Italian, Cuban, and Japanese offerings. Main courses might be potato-wrapped shrimp and seared mahi over local arugula, pistacchio-crusted rack of lamb, steamed red snapper with smoked oysters and ginger, and tenderloin of beef with peppercorns. *Entertainment three nights a week. Reservations essential. 340.714.6075. Five minutes west of Cruz Bay. D $$$*

EQUATOR

Stone steps wind up through bougainvillaea to the open-air dining level of this restored sugar mill at Caneel Bay resort. It's dark and romantic and some nights a soft steel pan duo entertains. The eclectic menu features

STONE TERRACE

The al fresco bar is designed in a broad "U" and locals and visitors belly-up to trade tales of their day's adventures. You can also dine at the bar and drink and/or dine at the little tables in the bar area. *Closed Mon. 340.693.9370. Across from the south end of Wharfside Village.*

WOODY'S SEAFOOD SALOON

Day and night this place is packed and you can eat until 1 a.m. "Body shots" are popular here. *340.779.4625. Across from First Bank.*

CORAL BAY RESTAURANTS & BARS
AQUA BISTRO

An inviting open-air bar marks the entrance to this popular Coral Bay outdoor restaurant. Well-spaced tables, shaded by umbrellas, are set in a quiet terrace. The varied menu includes everything from hamburgers and sandwiches to grilled steaks. There's live music Friday evenings and during Sunday brunch and one-of-a-kind shops on both sides of the terrace that are great for browsing. *340.776.5336. Rte. 107 at Coccoloba Shops. Brunch only Sun. LD $-$$*

ISLAND BLUES

This very casual eatery serves excellent food. Tables overlook the water from the bar area and more tables are on a gravel terrace at the water's edge. The varied menu offers burgers, salads, reubens, a great "build your own" grilled cheese, and even meatloaf. Check out the the daily soup, quesadilla, and sandwich special. The quesadilla might be a perfect blend of barbecued beef, cheddar cheese, and onions. The sandwich might be a blackened tuna with wasabi mayo. There's a popular happy hour and entertainment. *340.693.6800. Rte. 107, north of Coccoloba Shops. LD $*

SHIPWRECK LANDING

Dine casually al fresco on burgers, Caesar salads, fish 'n' chips, taco salads, amd pasta specials. Bands play Wednesday and Thursday evenings. *340.693.5640. Rte. 107, south of Coccoloba Shops. LD $*

SKINNY LEGS BAR AND RESTAURANT

Come to this casual, popular spot for a grilled portobello mushroom sandwich, or a turkey and Swiss sandwich, or great chili dogs, burgers, and grilled fish. Friday nights, there's often a band. Check out the "flip-flop" mobile. *340.779.4982. Rte. 10, east of the turn-off to Rte. 107. LD $*

CORAL BAY
FOR THE DAY

A trip to Coral Bay is a wonderful way to spend a day. Of course, if you are staying on this end of the island, these suggestions are right outside your door. Coral Bay is about a half hour, hilly, scenic drive from Cruz Bay, and the kicked-back atmosphere at this end of the island makes Cruz Bay look like Manhattan. Be sure to stop one way (or both) for a cone or smoothy at **Columbo's Best Smoothies** at the junction of Routes 10 and 20.

Don't be fooled by Coral Bay's sleepy first impression. There is plenty to do here with choices for everyone. Ride a horse or donkey along the beach or off into the hills. Call Dana at **Carolina Corral** *(340.693.5778)*. Or take a three-hour picnic and snorkeling cruise on **Serena Sea** *(340.779.4047)* or rent a dinghy or kayak or sunfish from **Crabby's Watersports** *(340.714.2415)*. They rent snorkeling gear, coolers, chairs, and fishing poles, too.

Or send everyone else out on a boat and relax with a therapeutic massage by Cathy Noonan *(340.693.9021)*. Speaking of serene, **Salt Pond Bay Beach** is about four miles south of Island Blues, a hike off Route 107 It is one of St. John's calmest and most peaceful beaches with good snorkeling along the eastern rocks.

For food or beverage, you can't go wrong at **Aqua Bistro**, **Skinny Legs**, **Island Blues**, or **Shipwreck Landing**. All have delicious food and a tasty selection of island drinks. If some shopping after lunch is in the plan, check out the many unique little shops near Skinny Legs and in the Coccoloba complex. Look for resortwear and cover-ups at **Bliss Boutique**, Argentinean leather goods and fine wool sweaters at **Pampa**, jewelry and fancy handbags at **Sugarapple**, and, for chips and dip, wine, or fresh veggies, stop in **Lilly's**, a full-service market.

CHAPTER 10

GREAT
ST. JOHN
SHOPPING,
OUTDOOR
ACTIVITIES

So I said to her,
"We're on vacation,
let's enjoy some outdoor activities."

"On St. John, shopping is an outdoor activity,"
she replied.

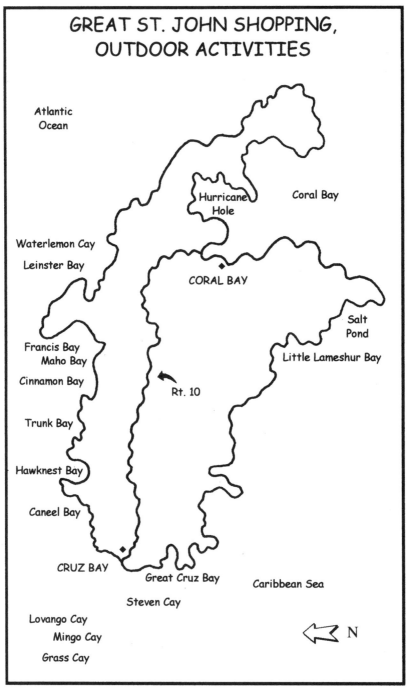

GREAT ST. JOHN SHOPPING

Shopping on St. John is a pleasure. It's almost entirely located in downtown Cruz Bay and there are many superb, one-of-a-kind places. Also, the town never gets ridiculously crowded the way it can in Charlotte Amalie. Cruz Bay shops are clustered in three areas. Mongoose Junction is a five-minute walk north of the ferry dock, and its beautiful stonework walls and arches make it one of the prettiest shopping areas anywhere. Wharfside Village is right on the water, south of the ferry dock. In between, "in the middle of town," are more stores. You can cover all of Cruz Bay on foot in about an hour or half a day, depending on what kind of shopper you are. And remember, just about anything you find can be shipped directly to your home.

MONGOOSE JUNCTION

BAMBOULA

Handsome armoires and cabinets show off a mix of clothing, textiles, Caribbean jewelry, and pottery. You'll find comfy, stylish island clothing for women; island shirts, pants, and shorts for men; and delightful bedspreads, cosmetics, cotton throws, and woven baskets. *340.693.8699.*

BEST OF BOTH WORLDS

Don't miss this outstanding gallery, a showcase of creativity. Look for appealing wire sculptures, watercolors, silver and gold jewelry, restful waterfalls, stunning clocks, colorful frogs, and some really whimsical creations. Go upstairs, where there's more of everything. *340.693.7005.*

BIG PLANET

Get ready for anything you might want to do outdoors with a stop in this multilevel store. You'll find swimwear, active wear, sunglasses, footwear, backpacks, luggage, and accessories from Patagonia, Teva, Jams World, Timberland, and Birkenstock for the whole family. *340.776.6638.*

BOUGAINVILLEA

Come here for a huge selection of upscale, stylish men's and women's clothing (shirts, pants, shoes, sweaters, purses, hats, bags) including Tommy Bahama and Axis, and a potpourri of appealing gift items. A smaller sister store is located at the Westin St. John. *340.693.7190.*

CANVAS FACTORY

Colorful canvas is the specialty here, fashioned into briefcases, purses, and satchels in all sizes. There's a superb collection of hats. *340.776.6196.*

CARAVAN GALLERY

A curving staircase leads upstairs to this display of unusual items from around the world. Look for monkeys, delicate silver and gold chains, exotic masks, sculptures, figurines, and other collectibles. *340.779.4566.*

CLOTHING STUDIO

Watch artists hand-paint everything from bathing suits to hats, T-shirts, sundresses, and cover-ups at this popular shop. *340.776.6585.*

FABRIC MILL

Head here for comfortable, casual island wear: linen and cotton pants, dresses, skirts, and tops in pastels and prints, plus sarongs, purses, tote bags, books, and unique gift items. *340.776.6194.*

R&I PATTON GOLDSMITHING

Look for delicate seahorse earrings, a trio of dancing lizards on a pin, a charm bracelet of tropical fish, a sea turtle pendant, plus unique chains and rings at this highly original gold and silver jewelry shop. *340.776.6548.*

ST. JOHN EDITIONS

Very upscale resort clothes are featured in this cozy shop, plus shoes and lacy Cosabella lingerie. *South of Mongoose Junction. 340.693.8444.*

WHARFSIDE VILLAGE

CRUZ BAY CLOTHING COMPANY

Racks are packed with an impressive array of bathing suits, cover-ups, and T-shirts, plus Fresh Produce and Jimmy Buffett shirts. *340.693.8686.*

DREAMS & DRAGONFLIES

Funky clocks, wind chimes, spirit rattles, candles, and casual women's pants and tops are just some of the items in this eclectic collection. *340.779.4212.*

EVERY TING

Watercolors, candles, greeting cards, island books, unique Caribbean gift items, plus Internet and e-mail access and a cappuccino bar make this a one-stop shopping pleasure. *Just south of Wharfside Village. 340.693.5820.*

FREEBIRD

This little shop is a good spot to pick up toe rings, ear swords, sterling silver and gold jewelry and the pale blue larimar stone. *340.693.8625.*

124

INTO THE BLUE
Don't miss this tiny shop filled with beautiful tiles, necklaces, pottery, ceramics, art glass, and much more, all by local artists. *340.777.1489.*

KHARMA
Stop in for lacy camisoles, strapless sundresses, slinky island wear, delightful purses, hats, sarongs, watercolors, and jewelry. *340.714.7263.*

ST. JOHN SPICE
The enticing aromas will draw you upstairs into this emporium of spices, coffees, teas, hot sauces, jellies, jams, and more. *340.693.7046.*

MIDDLE OF TOWN
NOW & ZEN
Look for exotic incense, silky tops and pants, purses, creams, and other treasures from the Far East. *340.714.1088.*

PINK PAPAYA
Just about everything here is in bright pastel solids and prints: oversize pillows, table linens, hand-painted dinnerware, ceramic bowls, coffee cups, stained glass ornaments, wacky sculptures, and even the colorful books and the Caribbean art by St. John artist M Lisa Etre. *340.693.8535.*

SILVERLINING
Lovely, handcrafted jewelry—bracelets, earrings, rings—plus appealing, interesting pottery are featured in this tiny spot. *340.693.7766.*

THYME
Two chairs mark the entrance to this inviting shop and its displays of stylish bathing suits, New Man clothes for men and women, sunglasses, sundresses, casual resortwear, purses, and pretty jewelry. *340.776.9453.*

OUT OF TOWN
CANEEL BAY RESORT SHOP
Definitely worth a stop is this terrific shop, stocked with resortwear for men and women, jewelry, pottery, current paperbacks, island books, plus colorful T-shirts, glassware, and beach towels emblazoned with the famous Caneel petroglyph logo. *Caneel Bay Resort. 340.776.6111.*

For shops in Coral Bay, please see page 120.

OUTDOOR ACTIVITIES

St. John is an outdoor paradise, above the water and below. There are terrific hiking and horseback trails, stunning beaches, calm swimming waters, and spectacular snorkeling. Luckily, two-thirds of the island is protected by the U.S. National Park Service. The Virgin Islands National Park includes almost all of the north shore beaches, some south shore beaches, and the waters around these beaches. Watersports come first in this chapter, followed by landsports.

BEACHES AND SNORKELING

Beaches are in geographical order, going clockwise around the island, starting at Cruz Bay. Also see the map at the beginning of this chapter.

SALOMON BEACH AND HONEYMOON BEACH

These small beaches are reachable only by boat or by trail. Salomon is just under a mile along the Lind Point trail that starts at the National Park Headquarters in Cruz Bay. It's been known to be "clothing optional" at times. Honeymoon is just a little farther along the trail, but can also be reached very easily from Caneel Bay Resort. **Snorkeling:** There are reefs on the left side of Salomon and between Salomon and Honeymoon. It can be quite shallow in places but you'll see lots of fish. *North shore.*

HAWKSNEST BAY

The reefs are close to shore at this narrow beach which gets crowded because it's so close to Cruz Bay. You can climb over the rocks at the west end of this beach to a small, more private beach. **Snorkeling:** Three reefs run out from the beach. Look for squid, damselfish, all kinds of angelfish, flatworms, and anemones. Snorkeling won't be good during north swells. *North shore.*

TRUNK BAY

Trunk Bay is a calm bay bordered by a gorgeous sweep of white sand fringed with sea grape and palm trees. This beach makes every list of the world's most beautiful beaches, so, unfortunately, it's no secret. Cruise ships send taxi-loads of passengers here. Trunk is still worth a visit, but to avoid the crowds come in the early morning or late afternoon. There's a $4 entrance fee from 7:30 a.m. to 4:30 p.m. for those 16 and older. **Snorkeling:** Look for the 225-foot, underwater, marked snorkel trail you can follow, with helpful signs identifying what you see. Trunk Bay is an excellent place to spot sea turtles and rays. Reefs full of fish are at both ends of the beach. Look for parrot fish, snappers, tang, and trunkfish and for caves and ledges at the western reef. *Snorkel trail, picnic area, snack bar, souvenir shop, snorkel rentals. North shore.*

CINNAMON BAY

At well over half a mile, this is the island's longest beach. It can be windy and is a good windsurfing spot. **Snorkeling:** It's great along the rocky east end. *Watersports center with snorkel and windsurfer rentals, scuba and snorkeling lessons, excursions, campground, restaurant. North shore.*

MAHO BAY

Beginning swimmers like the exceptionally calm waters and the fact that the water is so shallow for a long way out. There's no sign for this beach but you can see it from the road and you can park right at the edge of the beach. **Snorkeling:** A good place to catch sight of rays and turtles. *North shore.*

FRANCIS BAY

A long, narrow beach runs along this well-protected bay and the water is very calm. **Snorkeling:** This is a terrific snorkeling stop. Look for coral at the western edge, sea turtles out in the bay, octopus at the east end. You'll also see parrot fish, blue tang, and damselfish. *North shore.*

LEINSTER BAY/WATERLEMON CAY

The beach here is tiny and a bit rocky but Waterlemon Cay, at the eastern edge of big and beautiful Leinster Bay, is an outstanding snorkel spot. Beware of currents. **Snorkeling:** See turtles, stingrays, octopus, peacock flounder, sponges, seastars (starfish), and schools of parrot fish. *North Shore.*

SALTPOND BAY

You'll find fewer people at this wide beach than at many of the north shore beaches. **Snorkeling:** Look in the rocky areas for octopus and moray eels. This is also a good place to see angelfish, grunts, snappers, turtles, conch, and stingrays. *South shore.*

LITTLE LAMESHUR BAY

Expect to find few people at this remote beach. The drive is a bit rough but you end up right at the beach. **Snorkeling:** You'll see all kinds of fish among the eastern rocks and along the western shoreline. This is also a good place to catch a look at sea turtles and rays. *South shore.*

BOATING

DAY SAILS

You'll find a number of charter boats in Cruz Bay that will take you out for a half- or full-day sail or even a sunset sail.

Cruz Bay Watersports offers two great day sail adventures. There's a day sail to Virgin Gorda's Baths on the 60' *Island Time* every Monday, Wednesday, and Friday. This trip includes a continental breakfast, lunch, snorkel gear, and an open bar. There's also a day trip to Jost Van Dyke on the 40' powerboat *Blast* every Tuesday, Thursday, and Saturday. This trip includes snorkeling, lunch at Foxy's, and a stop in White Bay on the way home. *Per person rates: Virgin Gorda Trip $110 plus fee for customs, Jost Van Dyke trip $110 including fee for customs. Cruz Bay. 340.776.6234.*

Gypsy Spirit II offers a variety of sailing choices from snorkeling trips to sunset sails to wedding sails. This 35-foot DuFour yacht carries two to six guests and will happily take just two. The glass bottom dinghy is cool. *Per person rates: half-day $50, full-day $85. Sunset $45. 340.344.2211.*

Hurricane Alley features a 51' Hinkley, which takes a maximum of six people. A full-day sail includes a long sail, a buffet lunch at anchor, and an afternoon snorkel. They also offer an hour-and-a-half sunset cruise on the same sailboat and a half-day snorkel trip on a powerboat which stops at two snorkel spots on other islands. *Per person rates: Full day on Hinkley $130; sunset cruise $70 ($400 for a private sunset cruise); powerboat snorkel trip $65. Mongoose Junction. 340.776.6256.*

PARASAILING

Cruz Bay Watersports offers parasailing, an exciting and popular sport, from the Westin dock every hour. The cost is $65 to "fly" and $15 to ride in the boat. *Cruz Bay. 340.776.6234.*

RENTING POWERBOATS

When the water is calm, it can be a wonderful adventure to rent your own little powerboat and head out to an uninhabited island for the day. You can easily go to Grass, Mingo, or Lovango Cay, where there are little beaches, or to Whistling Cay, where there is the ruin of a house along a beach. You can even go to the British Virgin Islands (see page 94).

Ocean Runner Powerboat Rentals rents 22', 25', and 28' powerboats, each with a bimini, VHS radio, and cooler. You can hire a captain if you want, and rent snorkel and fishing gear. *$305-$675 per day (less off-season). Wharfside Village, Cruz Bay. 340.693.8809.*

Nauti Nymph rents 25', 29', and 31' power boats with bimini, VHS, cooler, and fresh water shower. You may captain yourself or hire a captain and, of course, rent snorkel gear. *$315-$425 (less off-season). Westin dock. 340.775.5066 or 800.734.7345.*

SEA KAYAKING/HOBIE CAT TOURS

The waters around St. John offer great sea kayaking and Hobie cat opportunities. There are cays to explore, and snorkeling spots to visit.

Arawak Expeditions rents kayaks and also has several guided excursions. Three-hour trips leave at 9 a.m. and 2 p.m. for a nearby cay and some snorkeling. Full-day trips depart at 10 a.m. for several uninhabited cays and snorkeling. They also have overnight and multiday camping trips. *$50 half-day, $90 full-day. Cruz Bay. 340.693.8312.*

Hobie Cat Tours offers the opportunity for the novice or experienced sailor to sail a Hobie to secluded cays and empty beaches away from the crowds that larger boats can't reach. Sail yourself or go with a very knowledgeable captain. Lessons available, too. *$70 half-day, $110 full-day. Cruz Bay. 866.820.6906 or 340.626.8181.*

WAVERUNNERS

The versatile **Cruz Bay Watersports** also offers guided waverunner tours in and around Pillsbury Sound. A single person waverunner is $75 and a two-person is $90. *Cruz Bay. 340.776.6234.*

DIVING
DIVING TRIPS

The underwater geography around St. John is shallow but there are still great 30' to 50' dives.

Cruz Bay Watersports takes certified divers out every morning for a two-tank dive. Pickup is 8:15 a.m. at the Westin Dock. You're in the water a few minutes later. The afternoon trip (1:15 p.m.) is a one-tank dive but they also take snorkelers and give scuba lessons. *Morning $85; afternoon $65; snorkelers $55; noncertified divers $95. Cruz Bay. 340.776.6234.*

DON'T KNOW WHAT TO DO?

The outdoor activities in this chapter are among the best St. John has to offer. However, if you don't really have a clue what you want to do or you want to do everything and need some guidance, then talk to professionals who can ask you key questions, tailor-make suggestions, and book almost any activity you can imagine. *St. John Adventures Unlimited at Gallows Point 340.693.7730. www.stjohnadventures.com; Activities Information Center at Mongoose Junction. 340.715.4944. www.bestofusvi.com*

LANDSPORTS

BIRD WATCHING

In winter months, bird lovers head to the Francis Bay Trail where they hope to spot a West Indian whistling duck, yellow-billed cuckoo, and some of the other more than 160 species of birds that live in this area.

HIKING

The National Park Service maintains over 20 hiking trails that lead through mountain forests and dry cactus and along old plantation roads to extraordinary beaches, overlooks with breathtaking views of neighboring islands, and historic sugar plantation ruins. Trails vary greatly in degree of difficulty and length and range from 10 minutes to three hours. Pick up a copy of the *Virgin Islands National Park Trail Guide* (count on trail times taking a little longer than stated) and be sure to bring plenty of drinking water with you. *National Park Visitor Center, Cruz Bay. 340.776.6201.*

HIKES WITH GUIDES

The National Park Service offers guided hikes down steep Reef Bay Trail, which includes a visit to sugar mill ruins and to ancient petroglyphs, and ends at a beach. Although signs along the way make this an easy trip to do on your own, the guided trip returns via boat while everyone else has a steep, two-mile hike back up the trail! Ask about full moon hikes. *Make reservations (hikes fill up fast). Mon., Thurs., Fri. $5 to head of trail, $20 guided hike, $15 boat ride back (all rates per person). 340.776.6201.*

HORSEBACK AND DONKEY RIDING

Go horseback or donkey riding along scenic trails up into the mountains or down to the beach. You can even go swimming with your horse! Carolina Corral Trail Rides offers two one-and-a-half-hour rides per day at 10 a.m. and 3 p.m. *$65 per rider (no credit cards). 340.693.5778.*

MOUNTAIN BIKE TOURS

Catch stunning scenery, visit beaches and historic ruins, and find splendid photo ops biking around the island. **Arawak Expeditions** offers tours for novice and expert cyclists. *$50 half-day; $90 full-day. 340.693.8312.*

TENNIS

Tennis anyone? There are good courts at Caneel Bay and the Westin St. John. If you are staying at either resort, court use is complimentary. If you are staying elsewhere, you may use the courts for a fee. Call and ask for the Tennis Shop. *Caneel Bay 340.776.6111; Westin St. John 340.693.8000.*

SECTION III

WATER
ISLAND
&
HASSEL
ISLAND

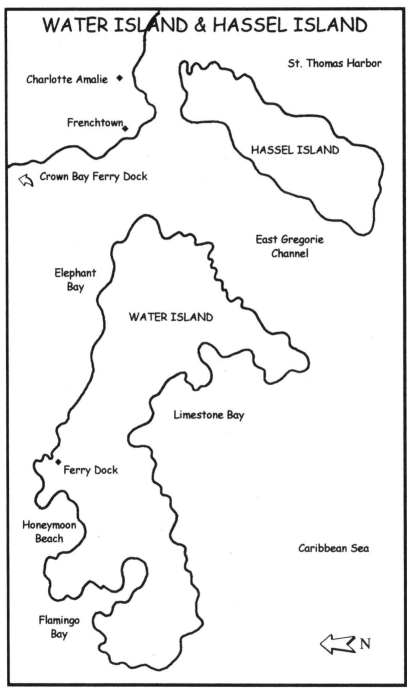

WATER ISLAND & HASSEL ISLAND

Charlotte Amalie ◆

St. Thomas Harbor

Frenchtown

HASSEL ISLAND

⇦ Crown Bay Ferry Dock

East Gregorie
Channel

Elephant
Bay

WATER ISLAND

Limestone Bay

◆ Ferry Dock

Honeymoon
Beach

Caribbean Sea

Flamingo
Bay

⇦ N

132

WATER ISLAND

Less than a half-mile off the south shore of St. Thomas lies Water Island, the fourth largest U.S. Virgin Island. Visiting Water Island is a great daytime adventure and vacationing on the island can be a perfect way to enjoy splendid isolation yet be just 10 minutes by boat from St. Thomas dining and shopping.

At just 492 acres, it's a miniature version of its sister Virgin Islands, quite hilly and with a curvaceous shoreline. The island is about two miles long and its width varies from about one-third of a mile to about 400 yards. The highest point is 294' and there are about 150 residents. Water Island has a pretty little curve of a beach known as Honeymoon Beach and another beach quite good for snorkeling. There are private residences and a few rental properties. The single store, the Pirate's Ridge Deli, does triple-duty as a bar and simple lunch and dinner restaurant. A floating pizzeria occasionally comes to the beach. Weekends, Heidi's Honeymoon Grill is a casual beach affair for lunch and dinner.

A DAYTIME BEACH ADVENTURE

For a gr___ ____ __ _____ adventure, head over to Crown Bay Marina, _____ __ ___ __ th the ferry to Water Island *(see page* _____ at docks next to Tickles _____ ow up soon enough _____ a takes five relaxing. (Bear in mind that weekdays the KonTiki Party Boat brings boisterous revelers to this beach for a few hours in the early afternoon.) On the other side of the island is coral Limestone Beach, which is rocky on the feet but great for snorkeling. This beach is a bit of a haul (a very long hike up and down) but you can sometimes find a ride. You can also hike to see the remnants of an old fort up on the hill. The views are terrific. Ask someone at the dock for directions to the fort. If you plan to hike around, bring plenty of drinking water.

If you are interested in a "guided" tour and want to do a little peaceful biking on Water Island, Water Island Adventures *(340.714.2186 or 340.775.5770)* is a great choice. They pick you up in their ferry and give you a tour of St. Thomas Harbor as they take you to the island. Once there, all bikes, equipment, water, etc., are provided as is an experienced guide. The tour ends up at peaceful Honeymoon Beach with a swim, a rest, and a cold drink. Not a bad day in paradise.

GETTING AWAY FROM IT ALL
FOR A WEEK, OR EVEN A MONTH

Staying on Water Island is a great way to enjoy delightful isolation without being truly isolated. Despite the fact that you are on an island with only 150 other people and one deli of nowhere." You can pretend to be you need fresh garlic. restaurant, you c pleasures

St. Thomas-Water Island Ferry Schedule

Monday-Saturday

From St. Thomas	From Water Island
6:30 a.m.	6:45 a.m.
7:15 a.m.	7:30 a.m.
8:00 a.m.	8:15 a.m.
10:30 a.m.	10:45 a.m.
12:00 noon	12:15 p.m.
2:00 p.m.	2:15 p.m.
3:00 p.m.	3:15 p.m.
4:15 p.m.	4:30 p.m.
5:15 p.m.	5:30 p.m.
6:00 p.m.	6:10 p.m.

NIGHT RUNS (Mon., Wed., Fri., Sat.)

9:00 p.m.	9:15 p.m.

Sunday (and holidays)

8:00 a.m.	8:15 a.m.
10:30 a.m.	10:45 a.m.
12:00 noon	12:15 p.m.
3:00 p.m.	3:15 p.m.

This schedule is subject to change. Call 340.690.4159 or 340.690.4446 or check the schedule at the dock in front of Tickles. Per person fare is $5 one-way (children $3), $9 round-trip (children $5), more for night runs and off-schedule runs. Inquire.

HASSEL ISLAND

It can be a bit of a hassle getting to Hassel Island but if you are the adventurous type, you might find it a lot of fun.

This is the island that sits right in the middle of St. Thomas harbor. Although there are a few private residences, most of the 135-acre island is part of the Virgin Islands National Park. Trails have not been maintained but if you want a bit of a rugged hike, it is possible to follow them. The National Register of Historic Places lists four spots on this island, including an old coal mining station and shipyard. These are unrestored and pretty much in ruin at the moment. Occasionally there are guided hikes. *Call 340.775.6238 or 340.776.6201, ext. 252 for information.* So how do you get here? Try calling the **Water Island Ferry** *(340.690.4159 or 340.690.4446).* Sometimes they will drop you off and pick you up, and if not, they can often put you in touch with someone who can.

PRACTICAL INFORMATION

ARRIVING

St. Thomas. You can fly to St. Thomas's Cyril E. King airport nonstop from many U.S. cities. **American** *(800.433.7300)* has nonstop service from Miami, New York/JFK, and Boston (seasonally). **Continental** *(800.231.0856)* offers nonstop service from Newark. **Delta** *(800.221.1212)* flies nonstop from Atlanta. **United** *(800.864.8331)* has Saturday nonstop service from Washington, D.C. and Chicago. **U.S Airways***(800.622.1015)* offers nonstop service from Philadelphia and Charlotte. In addition, **American** also flies direct from many U.S. cities to San Juan, Puerto Rico, for connecting flights to St. Thomas. If you are flying via San Juan and connecting to an American Eagle flight, bear in mind that you should get to your American Eagle gate early, because at the gate you will board a bus and be driven out to your plane. San Juan American Eagle connections can be somewhat chaotic and many people who must make a connnection prefer to make it in the States (for instance, nonstop to Atlanta or Miami, then nonstop to St. Thomas). If you need a flight from San Juan to St. Thomas, call **American Eagle** *(800.433.7300)*, **Cape Air** *(800.352.0714)*, or **LIAT** *(340.774.2313)*.

St. John. John has no airport and people fly to St. Thomas and then take a ferry to St. John. Ferries run regularly from both Charlotte Amalie and Red Hook on St. Thomas to Cruz Bay on St. John *(see ferry schedule, page 141)*. Charlotte Amalie is just five to ten minutes from the airport. The trip to Red Hook can take from 30 to 50 minutes, depending on traffic. If you are staying at Caneel Bay or the Westin St. John, you can check in at their airport check-in locations (just beyond the baggage carriage), and then be taken to their private ferries which go directly to the resorts. If several of you are traveling together to St. John, you may prefer to travel by private water taxi *(call **Dohm Water Taxi**, 340.775.6501)*.

BANKING AND ATMS

On St. Thomas, First Bank has four branches with ATMs, including one on the Waterfront in Charlotte Amalie and one at Port of Sale at Havensight. First Bank also has a branch and ATM in Cruz Bay on St. John. The Westin St. John has an ATM in their lobby and there is an ATM in Mongoose Junction on St. John. ATMs in the islands are less reliable than stateside ATMs, so don't always count on getting cash from them.

CAR RENTALS

Virtually all car rental agencies will pick you up at your resort and some resorts have rental agencies right on the premises. Cars run about $60 a day. On both St. Thomas and St. John, on-season, it is best to make your reservations well ahead of time to be sure of getting a car. Driving is on the left. **Car rentals on St. Thomas:** If you are staying at a full-service resort, you may not want to rent a car. The St. Thomas road system is hilly and trafficky and it is easy to get lost. Taxis are available everywhere to take you to and from restaurants, beaches, or even on a tour around the island *(see Taxis page 139 and pages 42-43)*. If you do decide to rent a car for a day of exploring or for your entire visit, try **Avis** *(800.331.1084, 340.774.1468)* which has locations at the airport, Havensight, and Marriott Frenchman's Reef; **Budget** *(800.626.4516, 340.778.9636)* which has locations at the airport, Havensight, and Sapphire Beach; **Hertz** *(800.654.3131, 340.774.1879)*, which has an airport location; or **Dependable Car** *(800.522.3076, 340.774.2253)*, a local and highly reliable rental agency three minutes from the airport. **Car rentals on St. John:** Many visitors to St. John will want to rent a car (usually a jeep), if not for their whole stay, at least for a day. It is fun to spend time on St. John visiting one beach after another and the main roads, although quite hilly, are well paved and clearly marked (beware that side roads are a completely different story--if you venture off the beaten track, be prepared for roads that turn into rocky messes leading nowhere). Call **Hertz** *(800.654.3131, 340.693.7580)*, **Varlack Ventures** *(340.776.6412)*, or **Lionel Jeep Rentals** *(340.693.8764)*, a local company with excellent service. *Note: If you are staying on one of the more remote locations on St. John, you will want to pick up your car in Cruz Bay before you check in.*

CRIME
On St. Thomas, act carefully, the same way you would in any city. Watch for pickpockets in Charlotte Amalie, especially when it is crowded. Don't walk at night; instead, drive or take cabs. On St. John, it is safe to walk around Cruz Bay at night. On both islands, don't leave valuables visible in your car, even if it is locked, and don't leave your wallet or jewelry lying about in your hotel room (if there is a safe in your hotel room, use it).

CURRENCY, CREDIT CARDS, AND TIPPING
The currency is the U.S. dollar. Most places take credit cards but you may encounter an occasional establishment that takes only cash or traveler's checks, so bring some along. Also, some establishments refuse to take American Express so be sure to bring a MasterCard or Visa. There is no sales tax. Restaurants vary, and usually no service is added, so tip as you would in the States (15%-20%); if 10% service is added, then make up the difference to get to 15%-20%; if 15% service is added, only add more if you want to. Most restaurants clearly state on the menu and the bill whether or not they include a service charge. If you are at all unsure, just ask.

DEPARTING

Visitors clear immigration and customs in St. Thomas and it is important to arrive at the airport two hours before your flight departure time. If you are flying via San Juan you will most likely clear customs again in San Juan.

DUTY-FREE SHOPPING

Each U.S. visitor, including children, can return with (or mail) $1,200 worth of duty-free imported goods from the U.S. Virgin Islands every 30 days. U.S. residents 21 years of age or over may return with 4 litres of liquor duty-free (5 litres if one is locally produced, such as Virgin Islands rum).

DOCUMENTS

Your airline will require picture I.D. when you check in at the airport. Although no identification is necessary to enter the USVI, **you will need a picture identification plus proof of citizenship**, such as a birth certificate or passport, **to depart the USVI. If you have a current passport, bring it. You will find that having a current passport makes the process of clearing customs and immigration much smoother and less problematic.** Also, once you see how close the British Virgin Islands are, you'll probably want to head there for a day and you MUST have a valid passport to enter the BVI.

DRIVING

First of all, it's on the left. Second, these are extremely hilly islands and the roads are steep and curvy. Be very careful when it rains. Islanders drive fast and tailgate. Try to ignore the tailgating or pull over and let them pass. Main roads are well paved but side roads aren't. This is particularly true on St. John. Also, buckle up. Seat belt use is law-enforced and the fine is $25.

INTERNET AND E-MAIL

Most hotels provide a computer in the lobby that guests may use either free or for a nominal charge. Many hotels have in-room data ports as well. To access e-mail, stop by a Cyber Cafe or a communication center. There are many on both islands. See page 93 for suggestions.

LODGING

There is an 8% hotel tax and some hotels add a 10% (or more) service charge. Don't assume that even the fanciest lodging on St. Thomas and St. John will equal the service, cuisine, and amenities one can expect to find in a full-service, luxury stateside resort. Remember, you are in the Caribbean. So relax, slow down, and enjoy the view.

PUBLIC HOLIDAYS

The USVI celebrate all major U.S. holidays. Banks and virtually all shops will be closed on these days. Carnival is a month long festival, but most activities occur during the last two weeks. On St. Thomas, these last two weeks bracket Easter Sunday. On St. John, Carnival ends on July Fourth.

SPECIAL NEEDS

Accessible Adventures *(866.282.7223, www.accessvi.com)* offers tours for guests that have mobility restrictions. On both St. Thomas and St. John these tours focus on historical sites and beautiful scenery. On St. John the **St. John Community Foundation** *(340.693.7600)* offers tours aboard an accessible van. At Trunk Bay there is **De-Bug**, an all-terrain vehicle that makes the trip from the parking lot to the water's edge much easier for visitors with mobility challenges. Call the Virgin Islands National Park Service *(340.776.6201)* for information. **DIAL-A-RIDE** *(340.776.1277)* offers transportation services and tours on St. Thomas for persons with disabilities. Persons with disabilities who wish to go diving can call **Aqua Center** *(340.775.6285)* or the **Admiralty Dive Center** *(340.777.9802)* on St. Thomas. For the most current list of ADA-compliant resorts and hotels, call the USVI Visitors' Bureau *(800.372.8784)* and ask for the most recent edition of the U.S. Virgin Islands Rates brochure.

TAXIS AND BUSES

For information on taxis and how they operate, see pages 42-43. If you want to call a taxi on St. Thomas, good taxis include **EverReady Taxi Service** *(340.473.7445)*, **Sunshine Taxi** *(340.775.1145)*, and **Asner Bellevue** *(340.776.0676 or 340.643.7849)*. On St. John, look for taxis by the ferry dock in Cruz Bay or call the Taxi Dispatcher *(340.693.7530)*. Most taxis offer shared rides. Private taxis, which are much more expensive, can be arranged on St. Thomas. At the airport, just ask the taxi dispatcher. Or call **Chris' Taxi Service** *(340.690.1581)*. VITRAN buses *(340.776.4844)* cover popular routes on St. Thomas. VITRAN buses run from 5 a.m. to 10:15 p.m. between Cruz Bay and Coral Bay/Salt Pond on St. John.

TELEPHONING AND CELL PHONES

The area code for the USVI is 340. When you are calling within the USVI, use the seven-digit number without the area code, even if you are calling from one U.S. Virgin Island to another. Many locals (boat trips, fishing trips, taxi drivers) have cell phones, and sometimes when you dial these numbers you will get an "out of range" recording even when the person is not out of range. Just try the number again. Your stateside cell phone will most likely work in the USVI. Call your provider. If you can bear it, try turning your phone off, especially if you came to the islands to "get away from it all."

TIME

The U.S. Virgin Islands are on Atlantic Standard Time, which is one hour ahead of Eastern Standard Time. However, the USVI does not switch to Daylight Saving Time and during these months the USVI are on the same time as the U.S. eastern time zone.

WEATHER

People often think that the farther south one goes, the hotter it gets. Not true! The USVI temperatures hover around 75 degrees in the winter, 85 degrees in the summer and the trade winds almost always blow. New York City can be much hotter in August than the USVI!

WEB SITES

For info on St. John and St. Thomas, go to www.usvitourism.com.

WHAT TO BRING

Sunscreen (the USVI are only18 degrees from the equator and the sun is strong all year long), bug repellent, casual clothes. In the evening at the nicer restaurants on St. Thomas, casual elegant resortwear is appropriate, including long pants and collared shirts for men. St. John is more relaxed, although Caneel Bay and the Westin St. John both require collared shirts and long pants for their fancy restaurants. Bring sturdy shoes if you want to hike and perhaps a light sweater as evenings can be cool any time of year.

KEY TO RESTAURANT SYMBOLS

"B" and "L" and "D" appear at the end of restaurant descriptions and indicate whether the establishment is open for breakfast, lunch, and/or dinner. Meal prices are similar to those in a large U.S. city. Dollar symbols indicate price ranges. Lobster is always expensive and appetizers and desserts can add surprising amounts to a bill.

$ = INEXPENSIVE $$ = MODERATE $$$ = EXPENSIVE

SUGGESTED READING. If you are a big reader, James A. Michener's century-spanning tale, *Caribbean*. For a humorous view of life in paradise, Herman Wouk's *Don't Stop the Carnival*. For those contemplating a life change, Sidney Hunt's *How to Retire in the Caribbean*. If you're going to Peter Island, Hugh Benjamin's *A Place Like This*—and get Benji to autograph it. If you're going to the BVI, Pam Acheson and Dick Myer's *The Best of the British Virgin Islands, Fourth Edition*. For pirate lovers, Fritz Seyfarth's *Pirates of the Virgin Islands*. For interested readers, Mark Kurlansky's *A Continent of Islands* or Jamaica Kincaid's *A Small Place*. If you are planning some serious exploring on St. John, Pam Gaffin's *Feet, Fins, and Four-Wheel Drive*. If Jost Van Dyke is in your plans, Peter Farrell's *Foxy and Jost Van Dyke*. Get Foxy to sign it.

INDEX

ABOUT THE AUTHORS

Since escaping from corporate life in Manhattan, husband and wife team Pam Acheson and Dick Myers have spent the last 15 years living in and exploring the Virgin Islands and Florida. Between them they have authored, written, and contributed to over 60 books, written articles for many national and international magazines, and have been featured guests on dozens of television and radio shows throughout the United States and the Caribbean. Their extremely knowledgeable, personal, reader-friendly guides to the U.S. Virgin Islands, the British Virgin Islands, and romantic Florida perennially rank among the best sellers for these destinations in the world. They reside in the Virgin Islands and Florida...and quite enjoy visiting Manhattan.